GEZA VERMES

The Resurrection

PENGUIN BOOKS

PENGUIN BOOKS

Published by the Penguin Group
Penguin Books Ltd, 80 Strand, London WC2R 0RL, England
Penguin Group (USA) Inc., 375 Hudson Street, New York, New York 10014, USA
Penguin Group (Canada), 90 Eglinton Avenue East, Suite 700, Toronto, Ontario, Canada M4P 2Y3
(a division of Pearson Penguin Canada Inc.)
Penguin Ireland, 25 St Stephen's Green, Dublin 2, Ireland
(a division of Penguin Books Ltd)
Penguin Group (Australia), 250 Camberwell Road,
Camberwell, Victoria 3124, Australia (a division of Pearson Australia Group Pty Ltd)
Penguin Books India Pvt Ltd, 11 Community Centre,
Panchsheel Park, New Delhi – 110 017, India
Penguin Group (NZ), 67 Apollo Drive, Rosedale, North Shore 0632, New Zealand
(a division of Pearson New Zealand Ltd)
Penguin Books (South Africa) (Pty) Ltd, 24 Sturdee Avenue,
Rosebank, Johannesburg 2196, South Africa

Penguin Books Ltd, Registered Offices: 80 Strand, London WC2R 0RL, England

www.penguin.com

First published 2008
1

Copyright © Geza Vermes, 2008

The moral right of the author has been asserted

Set in 12/14 pt Monotype Garamond
Typeset by Rowland Phototypesetting Ltd, Bury St Edmunds, Suffolk
Printed in England by Clays Ltd, St Ives plc

978-0-141-03005-0

Contents

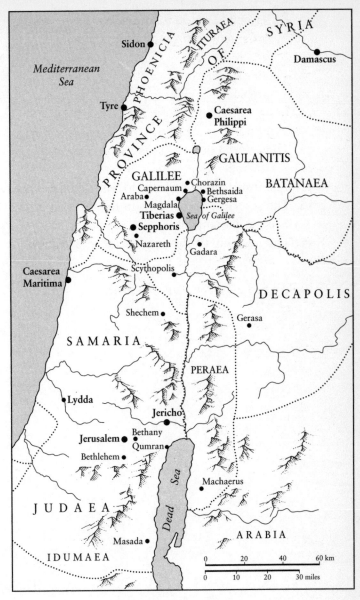

Palestine in the age of Jesus

Foreword

Each of the main topics of the New Testament focused on Jesus – the Nativity, the Passion and the Resurrection – confronts the historian with its own special problem. Complicated though its source material may seem, Good Friday, the culmination of the last few days of the life of Jesus, is in reality the simplest. Let me state plainly that I accept that Jesus was a real historical person. In my opinion, the difficulties arising from the denial of his existence, still vociferously maintained in small circles of rationalist 'dogmatists', far exceed those deriving from its acceptance. In my opinion, the scholar's task is simply to sort out and assess the evidence and determine the reasons why, when and by whom Jesus was arrested, tried and crucified. It is even possible to propose, with the help of known astronomical data, the most likely date for the event – Friday, 7 April AD 30 – corresponding to the eve of the Passover full moon.[1] Other scholars may disagree and advance a different date or shift the blame more on to the Jewish authorities than on the Roman governor, Pontius Pilate, but the debate will remain firmly set in the real world of history and law, Jewish and Roman.

The story of the birth of Jesus is surrounded by thicker haze and is less solidly grounded in fact. The information relating to time and space is more dubious and the legendary elements abound (virgin birth, miraculous star, angels and dreams). Nonetheless it is hardly questionable that shortly before the death of Herod the Great, a Jewish boy was born in Bethlehem or Nazareth, who, about thirty years later, following a brief public career, died on a cross and was buried not long after the fifteenth year (AD 29) of the reign of the Roman emperor Tiberius.[2]

The resurrection of Jesus 'on the third day' after his burial, followed by his ascension to heaven on the same day or after forty days, is of a quite different nature. Unlike the crucifixion, it is an unparalleled phenomenon in history. Two types of extreme reactions are possible: faith,[3] or disbelief.[4]

My own standpoint will differ from both of these as I intend to act as a detective seeking, as I did in my previous studies, to investigate what the authors of the New Testament actually say in their writings, and not what interpretative Church tradition attributes to them. The purpose of this volume is to unravel the true meaning conveyed by the evangelists, Paul and the other authors of the Christian scriptures and illuminate it with what we know from the Old Testament and all the relevant Jewish and Graeco-Roman literary and archaeological sources. Its aim is the construction of a tenable hypothesis, but ultimately it will be up to the readers to make up their minds. The dilemma to be confronted and resolved is how to reconcile the extreme importance ascribed to the resurrection by Christianity with the very limited amount of discernible interest in the subject in the authentic teaching of Jesus.

Not long ago an eminent Anglican churchman asked me what I was busying myself with and when he heard that after *The Passion* and *The Nativity* I was writing a book on the resurrection, he sagaciously observed, 'That seems to be the end of the story, except perhaps for the judgement.'

Prologue

The Christian notion of resurrection and its historical antecedents

Resurrection is unquestionably one of the most important and intriguing concepts of the Christian faith. Saint Paul, to whom this religion owes more than to anyone else, leaves his readers in no doubt in this respect:

If there is no resurrection of the dead, then Christ has not been raised; if Christ has not been raised, then our preaching is in vain and your faith is in vain ... If Christ has not been raised, your faith is futile (1 Cor 15:13–14, 17).

It is true to say that the emphasis laid on the notion of resurrection, and the centrality it is accorded in the Church's teaching, are unparalleled in the religions of antiquity. In the Judaism of the Old Testament resurrection made only a few, late and foggy appearances, probably not before the end of the third century BC. It was not asserted definitely before the time of the Maccabaean revolution in the 160s BC and from then on its acceptance grew slowly and remained far from universal. In its strict meaning, i.e. the revival of a corpse, it struck non-Jews in the Graeco-Roman world as at best a nice dream, but more generally as folly (*dementia*), according to Pliny the Elder's sharp remark.[1] Even in the Acts of the Apostles of the New Testament, when Paul preached 'the resurrection' in the

Areopagus of Athens, most of his philosophically educated listeners, Stoics and Epicureans, simply poked fun at his 'babbling' (Acts 17:18, 32).

Resurrection, or more precisely bodily resurrection, is definitely a Jewish idea. It entails the corporeal revival of the dead, the reunification of the spiritual soul and the material body of a deceased person. In the Hebrew Bible, resurrection first appears as a metaphor, symbolizing the rebirth of the nation. According to the mystical vision of the prophet Ezekiel, it depicts the figurative clothing with flesh of the dry bones of the people of Israel, and the blowing by God of the breath of life into the skeletal remains of a defeated, dispersed and exiled nation. The resurrection of the dry bones indicates something different from spiritual survival. It is not to be confused with the Greek (Platonic) concept of the escape of the soul from the prison of the body to proceed towards the Elysian Field of Heaven. It is not identical with the eternal life of the spirit. This idea of liberation is a familiar feature of the writings of Hellenized Jews of the Diaspora and the notion of eternal life without specifically implying a renewed presence of the body is also commonly attested in the Greek New Testament. These are ill-defined notions which must be handled with great care if confusion is to be avoided.

Another setting for the resurrection of the dead is provided by the awesome and majestic image of the final judgement when, at the end of the age known to man, Jewish and Christian religious visionaries imagine a universal roll-call of humanity by a blazing angelic trumpet. The dead will then be restored to their former bodies and face God or his representative, variously called the Messiah, the Chosen One or the Son of Man. The task of the final Judge will be to separate the resurrected into righteous sheep and wicked goats, and assign them eternal reward or eternal punishment. The righteous will be granted everlasting joy in the celestial abode and the wicked will be cast into the endless torment of a fiery hell. This universal settlement of accounts is the final stage of the doctrinal development in Judaism. An earlier version of the resurrection of the dead envisages only the revivification of the just, first and foremost the martyrs who in the course of a religious persecution have sacrificed their lives for the sake of Heaven. As the later Jewish rabbis would put it, they accepted agony and violent death for 'the sanctification of God's name'. In sum, resurrection preliminary to the great judgement pertains to eschatology, to the events of the end of times. This is tantamount to stating the obvious, namely that rising from the dead is alien to man's normal, historical experience.

While the Christian Church continues to proclaim belief in a universal resurrection and a new life in the age to come, it also firmly maintains that Jesus was raised from the dead in time past, on the third day after he had expired on the cross. In other words, the phenomenon of the dead Christ regaining life is claimed to have actually occurred in this world, before daybreak on a Sunday, probably on 9 April AD 30, if the dating of the crucifixion to the afternoon of Friday 7 April of that year is accepted. This belief turns resurrection – previously envisaged as either a metaphor or a future eschatological event – into a reality that occurred in a given place at a specific time. The basis of this innovative perception and the arguments supporting the resurrection belief will be scrutinized in the pages that follow, but in the meantime some further preliminary clarifications are needed.

In one sense, the resurrection of Jesus is presented by

the New Testament and the Church as a unique happening that can be dated and located. However, it is also linked to the eschatological raising of the dead of which, in St Paul's terminology, Christ's resurrection constituted the 'first fruits'. At the same time, according to the Old and New Testament sources, Jesus was not the only human being to rise from the dead. The scriptures refer to the resurrection of other individuals. The Old Testament prophets Elijah and Elisha resuscitated two children, and Jesus himself is reported to have brought back to life two others in the Synoptic Gospels (pp. 87–9) and a third one, Lazarus, in John (p. 90), not to mention two further miraculous stories connected with St Peter and St Paul (p. 91). The revival of a young bride in Rome, credited to the first-century AD neo-Pythagorean holy man Apollonius of Tyana, belongs to the same category.[2]

These stories about resurrection in general and the reviving of the dead by Jesus in particular will be examined in detail in Part II of this book, together with the doctrinal and theological considerations which fill the pages of the New Testament and especially the letters of St Paul. To give one example, words dealing with resurrection figure no less than nineteen times in 1 Corinthians, chapter 15. The opinion of the Jewish population of the late Second Temple period was more divided on the subject. The Pharisees were the only wholehearted champions of belief in bodily resurgence. When the ancient rabbis took over the Pharisaic legacy after the destruction of the Temple of Jerusalem in AD 70, they provided a niche for the doctrine of the resurrection in the Mishnah, Talmud, Midrash and Targum, but their interest in the faith in resurrection was not as prominent and exuberant as that of their Christian contemporaries.

The present study is essentially devoted to the evidence relating to the doctrine of the resurrection developed in the New Testament. However, it is impossible to understand the Christian scriptures without first inspecting their sources and models, the Hebrew Bible and early post-biblical Jewish literature not only as far as the resurrection imagery itself is concerned, but also in a broader sense regarding the ideas of life and death and even the underworld where, according to the Christian Creed, the dead Jesus descended before rising again on the third day.

I

Afterlife in the Jewish world
before Jesus

I

A bird's-eye view of human destiny in the Bible: From lost immortality to resurrection

Resurrection, the reversal of death, is presented by Christianity as the apogee of divine benevolence obtained for mankind by Jesus. Yet it is no more than second best among the possible options. Immortality, or escape from death, would have been the apex of all the possibilities, the dream of every human being ever since time began. The 'myth' of the creation, a sacred epic narrative included in chapters 2 and 3 of the biblical Book of Genesis, was meant to explain the fundamental phenomena affecting humanity. It is an attempt to account, in moral terms, for death or the loss of immortality, while ancient pagan epics attribute it to the caprice or jealousy of the gods.

The divine Potter of the Hebrews fashioned out of the dust of the ground the first creature, Adam, and shaped for him a female partner to keep him happy. The Creator installed both Adam and Eve in the glorious Garden of Eden and freely supplied them with all their needs. Their life was an endless holiday, with no obligation to work. They might, as it were, have lived happily for ever in Paradise, miraculously nourished by the fruits of the trees, among which stood the Tree of Life and the Tree of Knowledge. Death does not seem to have played a part in the original divine plan. But the first couple spoiled their blessed destiny of a joyful and immortal future when they allowed the Devil, or Serpent, to lead them astray, and transgressed the single restrictive rule that God had imposed on them: the prohibition to eat the fruit of the Tree of Knowledge.

The price they had to pay for what became in the theological jargon of the Church the 'original sin' was not only the forfeiture of an endless insouciance, but also the inevitability of death. The divine sentence proclaimed: 'In the sweat of your face you shall eat bread till you return to the ground, for out of it you were taken; you are dust and to dust you shall return' (Gen 3:19).

Later Jewish tradition and Pauline Christianity sought to apportion the blame for this loss of immortality between the three protagonists: the Devil, Adam and Eve. The male-chauvinist author of Genesis and the similarly inspired Jewish sage of the early second-century BC Jesus Ben Sira pointed the finger at Eve: she was the first to taste the forbidden fruit and enticed Adam to do the same. 'From a woman sin had its beginning and because of her we all die', lamented Ben Sira two centuries before Jesus (Ecclus 24:25). A little later, the author of the Greek Book of Wisdom philosophically assigned the primary guilt for the mortal fate borne by mankind to Satan, the source of all evil: 'Through the devil's envy death entered the world' (Wis 2:24). But in the eyes of St Paul, Adam, the forefather of the human race, bore full responsibility for the misery inflicted on his children: 'Sin came into the world through one man and death through sin' (Rom 5:12). Nevertheless, the first man was seen by Paul as the prototype of Christ, the last Adam, who remedied through his resurrection from the dead the lethal harm caused by the first Adam's foolishness.

Unlike the Jews of the Old Testament period, the inhabitants of ancient Mesopotamia seem to have simply refused to accept their mortal destiny. In the famous epic of Gilgamesh, the age-old creation myth of the peoples living in the lands between the Tigris and the Euphrates, the hero Gilgamesh, first faced with death when he lost his friend Enkidu, set out at once in search of the secret of immortality. But Utnapishtim – the Noah of the Babylonian flood legend – whom the gods spared from death as a reward for his saving from drowning the world and its inhabitants, declined to divulge the precious mystery. So Gilgamesh and the people after him had to acquiesce in their mortal condition. The traffic into the Mesopotamian underworld was one-way only – it was a 'land of no return' – and the same is true of the infernal region of the Bible and the Hades of the Greeks. 'Those who go down to Sheol do not come up', scripture tells us (Job 7:9).

For a long period, the biblical Israelites accepted that the common lot of mankind consisted in a gloomy, sleepy, semi-conscious and chilly endless existence in the abode of the dead. Apart from one allusion in the New Testament to Christ's preaching to the spirits gaoled in the netherworld, and unlike the Mesopotamian and Greek myths of the descent of various deities and heroes to Hades, Jewish tradition never describes any visit to the subterranean land of Sheol. The First Book of Enoch, where the antediluvian patriarch is shown the country of the dead, is a strange exception (see pp. 45–5). In mainstream Jewish thought, through the Old Testament period down to the beginning of the second century BC, all the humans of past ages were viewed as inheriting a diminished, joyless subsistence in a land of darkness into which they entered through the grave. God was consigned to oblivion in this 'land of forgetfulness' (Ps 88:12). He was unreachable among the shades; they neither worshipped him, nor could count on his helping hand. The various pagan religions honoured underworld deities, rulers of the realm of the dead: Nergal, Tammuz and Ereshkigal in Mesopotamia, Hades and Persephone among the Greeks and Pluto and Proserpina among the Romans. Jewish monotheism excluded this possibility and Sheol was in consequence a religionless, even Godless place: 'From the dead, as from one who does not exist, thanksgiving has ceased' (Ecclus 17:28).

This gloomy outlook on the destiny of the deceased – stoically accepted with blind resignation as the will of God – had a fortunate positive sequel; a renewed appreciation of this world with the recognition of the priceless religious potential of time. The true Creator was the God of the living and in the healthy realism of the ancient Hebrews religiousness could find expression only on this side of the grave. Hence the dream of the biblical Israelites – especially in the pre-exilic age, before the sixth century BC – was to enjoy a God-fearing, long and happy life amid their families and expect at the end, having reached the fullness of years, to join peacefully their predecessors in the ancestral tomb. According to the standard formula of the Old Testament, the Jewish kings 'went to sleep with their fathers' and were buried in the royal mausoleum. Prior to this pious reunion only those who were 'alive and well', rich or poor, kings or servants, had a chance to 'sing the Lord's praises' (Ecclus 17:28).

During the years of the Babylonian exile the idea of renewed existence suddenly sprung up at the national level following the loss of Jewish independence in 587 BC. The prophet Ezekiel's mystical vision of the revival of dry bones symbolized the resurrection from the dead of the people of Israel, really or figuratively slain by the armies of Nebuchadnezzar, king of Babel. But as well as this aspiration for collective renaissance we can find signs in post-exilic writings which show that individuals too yearned for escape from Sheol. In addition to man's innate dread of death and its consequences, the urge for flight from the underworld derived from the religious person's desire to go on praising, worshipping and giving thanks to the Lord. The Psalmist personified the devout Jew imagining himself in Sheol, and proclaiming there his wish to love God and confess his faith even beyond the grave. Did he just dream of a prolonged new life after death? No doubt, many of these exclamations can be explained as prayers uttered by the sick for deliverance from *premature* death, but occasionally the poet's eyes appear to transcend the perspective of the present life:

Nevertheless I am *continually* with Thee;
Thou dost hold my right hand.
Thou dost guide me with thy counsel
and afterwards thou wilt receive me to glory . . .
My flesh and my heart may fail,
but God is the rock of my heart and my portion *for ever*
(Ps 73:23–24, 26).

Moreover the traditional view, that in the hereafter all will be treated as equals, is replaced by a new vision with a distinction between the righteous and the wicked prevailing even in the land of the dead. Sheol is the home of the fools; only they are there to stay. But for the devout a ray of hope will shine: 'God will ransom my soul . . . for he will receive me' (Ps 49:14–15). By contrast, the Jews who have lived a devout life will reside with the Patriarchs. They will be brought to Abraham's bosom, to use a rabbinic phrase (*behiqqo shel Abraham*), the antiquity of which is guaranteed by its appearance in the New Testament (Lk 16:22). In short, during the centuries following the Babylonian exile an image different from death's dreamless sleep flickers over the Jewish religious horizon.

The new outlook developed along two separate paths in the post-exilic period (after 539 BC). It found its first formulation during the latter part of the third century, and gained strength in the course of the second and first centuries BC. It is attested on the one hand in the Hebrew Bible in the little Apocalypse inserted into the Book of Isaiah (chapters 23–27) and in chapter 12 of Daniel, and in the Book of Wisdom of Solomon among the Greek Apocrypha in the Septuagint on the other hand.

In Hebrew thought, victory over Sheol was revealed in the reanimation of the dead bodies of the righteous. The author of the Apocalypse of Isaiah rejoices: 'Thy dead shall live, their corpses shall rise, O dwellers in the dust, awake and sing for joy' (Isa 26:19). The wicked rulers of past ages would reap destruction as their just deserts, and their memory be blotted out for ever (Isa 26:13–14). In this vision, resurrection is envisaged as the reward reserved for the just. At the next stage, in the Book of Daniel, it becomes universal and was followed by divine judgement remunerating the good and annihilating the godless: 'And many of those who sleep in the dust of the earth shall awake, some to everlasting life, and some to shame and everlasting contempt' (Dan 12:2).

However, beside the Palestinian Jewish concept of the restored unity of body and soul, the reawakening of the 'sleepers in the dust', Hellenized Jews, such as the author of the Greek Wisdom of Solomon, shun the idea of a renewed bond between the soul and the body and prefer to envisage the immortality of afterlife as the liberation of the spirit from the prison or the 'earthly tent' of the flesh (Wis 9:15).

The idea of an afterlife victorious over Sheol, be it through the resurrection of the body or the deliverance of the immortal soul, was not universally embraced by the Jews at the turn of the era. As we shall see, it was a belief characteristic of the Pharisees in the age of Jesus, but the Sadducees, the conservative priestly aristocracy of the late Second Temple period, firmly adhered to the traditional concept of the finality of death. 'Do not forget, there is no coming back', declared Jesus Ben Sira, who also testified to a quasi-fatalistic outlook: 'This is the end for all flesh decreed by the Lord' (Ecclus 38:21; 41:4).

It is in this context of contradictions that we will have to confront the New Testament statements of Jesus and of his followers regarding the resurrection from the dead. However, before envisaging these lofty ideas, we will need a deeper grasp of ancient Judaism's perception of death with its sequels, the grave, Sheol and afterlife, as reflected in the literary legacy of the Jewish inhabitants of the Graeco-Roman world.

2

Death and its sequels in ancient Judaism: Paving the way for resurrection

Sometimes one can be forgiven for stating the obvious: no one can be resurrected unless he has died first. Consequently, before reflecting on the meaning of resurrection we must grasp what cessation of life signified to Jews two thousand years ago. With this in mind, let us focus on the blurred and sketchy pictures of death, the grave and the underworld of Sheol. In fact, without a full understanding of these concepts we cannot even begin to perceive what the early Christian writers tried to convey when they told their readers about Christ's rising from the dead. Here are the details transmitted by the New Testament. Jesus *died* on the cross. His body was immediately *buried* in a *tomb*. Some forty hours later, several women friends came to complete the *funeral rites*; the anointing of his body had had to be postponed because of the onset of the Sabbath. Between death and resurrection, Jesus in spirit descended to the *underworld* to preach to the spirits imprisoned there. On the third day after his death, his *resurrected body* appeared to his apostles, although they first believed it was a *ghost*.

For the religious Jew of the biblical age life originated with the spirit breathed by God into the first human shape that, according to Genesis, he had made of dust or clay. As a result, Adam became a *nephesh hayah*, a 'living soul', an animated being. When this breath of life departs, the living being turns into a 'dead soul', a *nephesh met*. The person remains identifiably the same, but starts a different, diminished, inferior state of existence.

Out of respect for the deceased person his relatives washed, clothed and buried the body. In earlier times no coffins were used. Embalming, an Egyptian custom, is not attested in the Jewish Bible except for the patriarchs Jacob and Joseph who died in Egypt (Gen 50:2, 26). By New Testament times, in connection with Jesus, reference is made of the application of spices to the body (Mk 16:1; Lk 24:1) and more specifically a large quantity of myrrh mixed with aloes is mentioned (Jn 19:39).

An unburied corpse left as prey for birds and scavenging dogs was seen as the worst fate that could await a man. It is alluded to in the curse of Deuteronomy (28:26), pronounced on those unfaithful to the covenant: 'Your dead body shall be food for all the birds of the air, and for the beasts of the earth, and there shall be none to frighten them away.' The duty of the living, in the first instance the sons of the dead person, was to lay the body to rest. They buried it in the ground or deposited it in a natural or manmade rock cavity, the opening of which was protected against intruders by a heavy stone. Persons of means were placed in family tombs, like the Hebrew patriarchs in the cave of Macpelah, near Hebron. Sarah was buried there by Abraham, Abraham by his sons Isaac and Ishmael, Isaac by Esau and Jacob, and Jacob by Joseph, who repatriated the remains of his father from Egypt to Canaan.

About the end of the Old Testament period and in the age of Jesus, wealthy Jews constructed elaborate funerary monuments, often decorated and bearing commemorative inscriptions of the dead. Some of the rock tombs contained an antechamber where the body remained until the flesh had decomposed. Then the bones were collected and placed in containers, mostly made of limestone and known as ossuaries or bone boxes. The name of the deceased was often scratched or engraved on them and they were kept in rock chambers inside the tomb. The entrance of the tomb, as is also attested in the case of Jesus, was closed with a large round stone. According to the Gospel of Mark (Mk 16:3), the women who visited Jesus' grave at dawn on the Sunday after the crucifixion anxiously asked themselves whether they would be strong enough to roll the stone away.

In ancient Judaism's cultic dichotomy of the ritually pure and impure, dead bodies and everything associated with them belonged to the domain of the unclean, and had to be kept at a definite distance from anything or anybody associated with the holiness of the divine. Since a corpse was, as it were, 'contagious', those entrusted with worship had to avoid contact with it. Hence Jewish Temple personnel (Lev 21:1–4), like the priest and the Levite in the parable of the Good Samaritan (Lk 10:30–36), as well as the Nazirite votaries committed to the strictest adherence to purity rules (Num 6:6–7), were forbidden to touch a dead body and even to attend funerals except when the dead was a very near kin (father or mother, a son or a daughter, a brother or an unmarried sister). The effect of uncleanness was temporary; it lasted one week, and could be removed by means of two ritual purificatory baths, one on the third and the other on the seventh day. The Bible orders that a person condemned to death by a court should be buried on the day of his execution before sunset (Dt 21:22–23), as happened to Jesus, too. It may be taken for granted that the same rule applied in cases of natural death as well. All the regulations relating to dealings with dead bodies derive from the demands of primitive hygiene in a country with a hot climate.

For most Jews of the Old Testament period – the exceptions belong to the last two hundred years of the pre-Christian era and to the first century AD – the grave marked the final end of a man's story. Death was seen as inescapable and universal, or almost; the two biblical exceptions being the antediluvian patriarch Enoch and the prophet Elijah. Death is portrayed as the shepherd of all humans, whose flock is destined to the underworld (Ps 49:14). Death is 'the way of all the earth'; it cuts down the greatest like King David (1 Kings 2:1), just as it does the humble poor man. They all share the unending 'sleep of death' (Ps 13:3). Before the idea of resurrection was first mooted, the poetic author of the Book of Job wrote:

> But man dies and is laid low;
> man breathes his last, and where is he? . . .
> Man lies down and rises not again,
> till the heavens are no more he will not awake,
> or be roused out of his sleep (Job 14:10–12).

For the down-to-earth Jew of the biblical era, death was simply the common heritage of all the living. Christians brought up on the idea of resurrection and heavenly (or infernal) afterlife may be shocked to the core by the casualness of the biblical sage:

For the fate of the sons of men and the fate of the beasts is the same; one dies, so dies the other. They all have the same breath; and man has no advantage over the beasts . . . All go to one place; all are from the dust, and all turn to dust again (Eccl 3:19–20).

Being laid to rest in the grave, the 'dead soul' begins a new, transformed and final stage of existence in the underworld, the Sheol of the Bible, identical with the Hades of the Greeks. Sheol was imagined to be in the depth of the earth, the opposite of high heaven (Isa 7:11),[1] a land of doom, chaos and deep darkness, from where there is no return (Job 10:21–22). Sheol is compared to a fortified city whose gates are locked and reinforced with iron bars.

Two great poets, the prophets Isaiah and Ezekiel, offer highly colourful and picturesque descriptions of the entry of dead persons to this underworld. The all-powerful sovereign of Babylon is taunted on his arrival in Sheol by the vanquished kings whose remains lie in peace in their tombs, while the body of the Babylonian tyrant is cast away and trodden underfoot.

Sheol beneath is stirred up to meet you when you come,
it rouses the shades, to greet you . . .
all who were kings of the nations.
All of them will speak and say to you:
'You have become as weak as we!
You have become like us!'
Your pomp is brought down to Sheol,
the sound of your harps;
maggots are the bed beneath you,
and worms are your covering (Isa 14:9–11).

On earth, even the trees exult: 'The cypresses rejoice at you, the cedars of Lebanon, saying, "Since you were laid low, no hewer comes up against us"' (Isa 14:8). Sheol is the great equalizer, Ezekiel tells us. Even the proud Pharaoh of Egypt is finally cut down by the Lord God and brought low there in the midst of all the fallen peoples (Ez 32:19–32).

In biblical Jewish thought the dead do not vanish and turn into nothingness. They become emptied and weakened shades (the *rephaim*) who, incapable of producing normal sounds, communicate with hushed squeaks: 'Your voice shall come from the ground like the voice of a ghost, and your speech shall whisper out of the ground' (Isa 29:4).

Ancient Jewish magic and superstition offered a means to communicate with the inhabitants of Sheol. Ghosts were thought to possess knowledge potentially useful to the living, as long as the latter found a way to contact them by means of necromancy, entailing the use of a medium or a wizard. Necromancy is prohibited by the Mosaic Law under pain of death by stoning (Lev 20:27). Yet the Torah notwithstanding, the practice survived, and a fascinating account about King Saul summoning up the recently deceased prophet Samuel with the help of a medium illustrates both necromancy and the ancient Jewish ideas about a shade, or ghost (*'ov*).

Necromancy is a subdivision of the art of obtaining secret information that exceeds ordinary human faculties. The first Israelite ruler, Saul, intent on reading the future when he had to engage in combat with the Philistines, found that the permitted media (dreams, divination by the priestly Urim and prophecy) were useless. So he got hold of one of the rare clandestine necromancers still in the country after his earlier royal decree of expulsion of all the mediums and wizards. This woman, from the village of Endor, obeyed the king's order to bring up Samuel from Sheol. She saw his spirit, referred to as 'a god' (*'elohim*), rising out of the earth, looking like an old man wrapped in a robe. Saul recognized him as the prophet Samuel. The shade complained about being 'disturbed', woken up from his sleep, and in his bad-tempered mood shattered the king's last hope by announcing that next day Saul himself, together with his sons and the whole army of Israel, would join Samuel in the kingdom of the dead (1 Sam 28:8–19). The two main points that emerge from this story are that the shade summoned from Sheol was believed to have kept his recognizable shape, that of 'an old man', his individuality and to some extent his ability to think and to communicate with others. Outwardly, he appeared just as he was prior to his death and Saul had no doubt about whom he was seeing. The apparitions of the risen Jesus differ from that of Saul. Neither his disciples, nor Mary Magdalene, are said to have recognized him until he identified himself to them. Nevertheless, notwithstanding their surviving intellectual ability, the shades prefer to remain undisturbed and enjoy the deep sleep of death.

How did the idea of Sheol affect the outlook on life of the pious Jew? Absence of a second chance invested life on earth with a unique value. All good things happen to man between his birth and his death and the practice of religion is restricted to the here and now. Since only the living thank God (Isa 38:19), the days of this life are priceless. As reward for piety was expected before death, a kind of religious hedonism, consisting of eating, drinking and taking pleasure, was preached by the wise men of the Old Testament (Eccl 3:13). In lieu of mortification and asceticism, the Bible fully encourages the Jew to take delight in his days.

Go, eat your bread with enjoyment,
and drink your wine with a merry heart;
for God has already approved what you do.

Let your garments be always white;
let not oil be lacking on your head.
Enjoy life with the wife you love,
all the days of your vain life,
which he has given you under the sun.
Whatever your hand finds to do, do it with your might;
for there is no work or thought or knowledge
or wisdom in Sheol, to which you are going (Eccl 9:7–10).

Ecclesiastes, anticipating Horace's *carpe diem*,[2] preached a kind of Epicurean philosophy approved and blessed by God. Yet while having such an exclusive value placed on everyday existence strengthened practical religion, through emphasis on the service of God by the sanctification of every single act of life, it necessarily contained also a seed of discontent. A man with eyes to see could not help noticing that the principle underlying biblical Judaism would not withstand scrutiny. After all, the devout observer of all the precepts of the God-given Torah was not invariably rewarded, nor was the constant lawbreaker always chastised. Contrary to the assertion of Proverbs 3:33, the Lord's curse was not perpetually on the house of the wicked, and he did not continuously bless the abode of the righteous. Could one really believe in the splendid divine proclamation of Deuteronomy?

If you obey the commandments of the Lord, . . . you shall live and multiply and the Lord God will bless you . . . But if your heart turns away, . . . you shall perish . . . I have set before you life and death, blessing and curse; therefore choose life, that you and your descendants may live, loving the Lord your God, . . . for that means life to you and length of days, that you may dwell in the land which the Lord swore to your fathers . . . to give them (Dt 30:16–20).

The wise man knew from experience that real life did not mirror the ideals sketched by the lawgiver. Good health, peace and divine protection were not necessarily the wages of the law-abiding Jew. We need only read the sapiential and prophetic books of the Bible to discover that the devout were frequently sick, penniless and abused while the godless led a carefree and luxurious existence. The Psalmist's complaint, 'How long shall the wicked exult?' (Ps 94:3), was echoed by Jeremiah's indignation, 'Why does the way of the wicked prosper? Why do all who are treacherous thrive?' (Jer 12:1).

Ecclesiastes and Job went further and attacked head-on the official preaching of Deuteronomy about the mandatory prosperity of the virtuous and the inescapable comeuppance of the sinners. The sage Ecclesiastes phlegmatically remarked: 'In my vain life I have seen everything; there is a righteous man who perishes in his righteousness, and there is a wicked man who prolongs his life in evil-doing' (Eccl 7:15). Job, on the other hand, the prototype of the traditional idea of the religious man, rebelled with dramatic acuity. He was blessed by God, had seven sons and three daughters, seven thousand sheep, three thousand camels, five hundred yoke of oxen, five hundred she-asses and innumerable servants. Then all of a sudden he lost everything, possessions and children, and on top of it all, he was inflicted with a horrible and painful skin disease. Yet despite his misery, he continued to praise and worship God. His friends tried to demonstrate that he must have done something wrong, but Job tenaciously went on protesting his innocence. Even though at the end of the story, an editor of the book endeavoured to defend the status quo by restoring Job to his former condition, giving him another seven sons and three daughters, and doubling his original wealth, he could not remove the large question mark placed by the poetic author against the accepted formulation of the traditional religious wisdom.

The weakness of this formulation was further stressed when in the exilic age the idea of the vicarious punishment of sins was attacked by the prophets Jeremiah and Ezekiel. They both cited the proverb, 'The fathers have eaten sour grapes, and the children's teeth are set on edge' (Jer 31:29; Ezek 18:2), implying that innocent later generations could be chastised for the wrongdoings of their elders. They declared it untenable and insisted on personal responsibility: 'Behold, all souls are mine; the soul of the father as well as the soul of the son is mine: *the soul that sins shall die*' (Ezek 18:4; see Jer 31:30).

Contradictory attitudes stood side by side until an unprecedented historical phenomenon – martyrdom – reinforced the doubts of thinking Jews. Jews of the Maccabaean period showed a willingness to sacrifice their lives rather than deny their faith. Their death was not a punishment for betrayal of the Law; on the contrary, they died because of their attachment to it, and this revolutionary novelty opened the door to a fresh representation of afterlife, envisaged henceforth either as the survival of the immortal soul or as the resurrection of the body.

However, before turning the searchlights on the question of the resurrection expected at the end of times, we ought to cast an eye on the exceptions listed in the Bible and post-biblical Jewish literature concerning the revivification of the dead or escape from the underworld by means of divinely engineered assumption or ascension to heaven.

3

Biblical and post-biblical antecedents of the resurrection and ascension of Jesus

While the Hebrew Bible maintains that death and Sheol are the unavoidable destiny of mankind, it nevertheless records a few exceptions to the rule, and post-biblical Jewish literature slightly lengthens the list by adding two further cases. One escape route from the perpetual sleep of the underworld was through recall to life soon after man's last breath, before, as it were, he had time to reach Sheol and settle in.[1]

Assumption or ascension with the help of God was another means to escape Sheol. Both the concepts of revivification and rising above the human sphere are significant for the student of the New Testament. The former exemplifies the reanimations recorded in the New Testament, and the latter serves as the prototype of Jesus' ascent to heaven depicted by Luke in his Gospel and the Acts of the Apostles and also stated in the longer ending of Mark.

The resuscitation of a recently deceased person may be classified as the highest achievement of religious healing. The Books of the Kings recount how the wonderworking prophets, Elijah and Elisha, brought back to life two young boys, the children of the widow from Zarephath and of a wealthy woman of Shunem, both generous benefactresses of the prophets. The method of raising the dead is similar in both cases and consists not just in words of command or bodily contact, but in a kind of total identification with them in order to reintroduce breath into their corpses by means of a shamanistic kiss of life.

In the case of the son of the widow from Zarephath, Elijah laid the boy on his bed and stretched himself on him three times; as a result, the child was revived (1 Kings 17:17–22). According to the Greek version of the passage, instead of stretching himself on the boy, the prophet breathed thrice on him. The Aramaic translation is equivocal, as the verb employed can mean either to stretch himself or to sneeze. The resuscitation of the son of the Shunemite woman by Elisha is more colourfully sketched. First Gehazi, Elisha's servant, was dispatched to revive him by waving above the boy the prophet's staff, but this was of no avail. Next, Elisha lowered himself on the child and touched with his mouth, eyes and hands the mouth, eyes and hands of the boy, seeking to warm up his body. Then he stretched himself on him once more and the child returned to life after sneezing seven times (2 Kings 4:18–37).[2]

In both episodes, the narrators purport to convey stories of real revivals that occurred in time and space. The boys were dead, but thanks to the intervention of the prophets began to live again. The author of Ecclesiasticus, singing the Praises of Famous Men, expressly notes that Elijah 'raised a corpse' and brought it back from Hades (Ecclus 48:5).[3] One would expect the heroes of such events to become notorious, but no detail relating to their later life has been preserved either in the Bible or in post-biblical sources. They, like the individuals resuscitated by Jesus in the Synoptic Gospels and St Paul in the Acts of the Apostles, promptly disappear from the scene.

Elisha's name is linked to another case of miraculous resurrection, but it is attributed not to the living prophet, but to his relics – his bones – which were buried in a cave. According to the biblical account of the story, members of a funeral procession, while trying to escape a band of marauders, cast into Elisha's tomb the body they were carrying to the burial place. But as soon as it touched the prophet's remains, it miraculously revived and walked away (2 Kings 13:20–21). In his *Jewish Antiquities* Flavius Josephus (AD 37–*c.* 100) recounts essentially the same tale, except that in his version the man was murdered by the robbers and his body was thrown by them into the prophet's grave (*Ant* 9:183).[4] In his vignette dedicated to Elisha, Ben Sira also puts into relief the prophet's wonderworking powers: 'Nothing was too hard for him, and when he was dead, his body prophesied. As in his life he did wonders, so in death his deeds were marvellous' (Ecclus 48:13–14).

In sum, it should be stated that in the framework of popular prophetic Judaism, in which the curing of the sick occupied an important place, the phenomenon of resurrection, the restoration to life of a person recently deceased, in no way appeared to be out of place.

Besides resurrection, ascension or assumption, a miraculous transfer of the deceased to the supraterrestrial world provides another way to be exempted from the common fate of humankind. A person may be translated bypassing death completely, or after a quasi-instantaneous revival that followed departure from among the living. Prior to Jesus, the Hebrew Bible lists two cases of direct transfer, Enoch and Elijah, and Jewish tradition adds a further two, Moses and Isaiah, with the difference that their elevation happens after death.

The assumption of the antediluvian patriarch Enoch is alluded to in mysterious, elliptic style in Genesis 5:24: 'And

Enoch walked with God; and he was not, for God took him.' In the earliest comment on the verse we are told that it was on account of his righteous behaviour that God took Enoch to himself. Ben Sira stresses the patriarch's piety: 'Enoch pleased the Lord' (Ecclus 44:16) and so do the Septuagint and the Targums of Genesis 5:24: 'Enoch was well pleasing to God' (LXX); 'Enoch walked in the fear of the Lord' (Onkelos); 'Enoch served before God in truth' (Fragmentary Tg, Ps.-Jonathan and Neofiti). However, a later rabbinic view contests this positive assessment and asserts that the name of Enoch was inscribed in the scroll of the wicked and that this was why God had taken him, or that he was sometimes good and sometimes bad so God decided to snatch him while he was righteous (GenR 25:1).

The second half of the biblical verse, 'and he was not, for God took him', is explained by some as the transfer of the living Enoch from among 'the sons of men' (Jub. 4:23) or from 'the inhabitants of the earth' (Ps.-Jon. on Gen. 5:24) to a far distant place, 'beyond the land of Parwaim' (1QGen. Ap. 2:23), or to 'the ends of the earth' (1 En 106:8), where his son Methuselah was able to visit him. However, according to Jubilees 4:23 he was carried by angels to the 'garden of Eden', a place of ill-defined location, possibly lying somewhere between heaven and earth. A second interpretation firmly sets Enoch in the celestial realm. The Slavonic Enoch or the Second Book of Enoch makes its hero visit the seven heavens and Targum Ps.-Jonathan (Gen 5:24) portrays him as elevated to the firmament to act as God's secretary and given the name Metatron, 'great scribe'.[5] Irrespective of the explanation one adopts, Jewish Bible exegesis and folklore identify Enoch as the first human to be spared from a descent to the underworld. He needed no resurrection as he was transferred alive to paradise or heaven.

The biblical narrator also describes the elevation to the celestial sphere of the living prophet Elijah, witnessed by his disciple Elisha, who had inherited his spirit and his miracle-working mantle. Elijah rose upwards in a chariot of fire drawn by fiery horses in the midst of a whirlwind. Josephus, generally inclined to play down the miraculous in scripture, prefers to speak of the disappearance of Elijah and Enoch rather than their ascension to heaven (*Ant* 9:28), and even the Greek Bible puts an 'as it were' before stating that Elijah was lifted on high.

Biblical and post-biblical Jewish tradition maintains the reality of Elijah's elevation as it attributes to the *returning* prophet an important eschatological function, the preparation of the day of the Lord by reconciling fathers and children (Mal. 4:5; Ecclus 48:10). Indeed, Jesus himself was associated by some of his contemporaries with the new Elijah (Mk 8:27; Mt 16:14; Lk 9:19), and the evangelists themselves acknowledged John the Baptist as Elijah *redivivus* (Mk 1:2; Mt 11:10; Lk 7:27).

Further biblical figures credited with assumption or ascension in post-biblical Judaism are Moses and Isaiah. In the case of Moses, Deuteronomy 34:5 expressly asserts that he actually died after he had been permitted to view the promised land from the top of Mount Nebo in Transjordan. According to the Bible no human eyes witnessed the end of Moses, and it was God who buried the Lawgiver in a secret place known only to himself. Without specifying their identity, the Greek Bible attributes the laying to rest of Moses not to God alone, but to an anonymous plurality: 'and *they* buried him'. Later tradition suggests that angels performed part of the ceremony. The New Testament, in turn, alludes to a fight between Satan and the archangel Michael for the body of Moses (Jude 9) and the Pseudo-Jonathan Targum (Dt 34:6) colourfully depicts the funeral rites of the Lawgiver. The chief angels Michael and Gabriel prepared the bed, which was decorated with diamonds and precious stones; Metatron, Yophiel, Uriel and Yephiphiah placed the body of Moses on it and God carried the bed to its resting place in the valley four miles away, opposite Beth-peor. However, according to the Church Father Origen, a Jewish writer dating to the first century AD followed up the burial with Moses' transfer to heaven. The proof derives from the title of the work, The Assumption of Moses, for unfortunately the end of the story is missing from the single Latin manuscript which has preserved this apocryphon. The implication is that after it had been laid to rest by the angels and God, the body of Moses was revived and lifted up to heaven.

There is no biblical evidence describing the death and the afterlife of the prophet Isaiah, but rabbinic tradition knows about his murder. Fleeing from Manasseh, the wicked king of Israel, Isaiah concealed himself in a hole within a cedar tree, but the king ordered the tree, together with the prophet inside it, to be sawn into two (ySanh 28c; bYeb 49b). An apocryphon, the Ascension of Isaiah, written by a Jewish author in the first century AD and re-worked by a Christian editor, recounts that after his execution the prophet journeyed upward, as Enoch did before him, and was led by an angel through the seven heavens (chapters 7–9).

In sum, pre-Christian Judaism was aware of some peculiar cases where death was not the end of the story for certain important individuals. We are not told what happened to the two children resurrected by Elijah and Elisha, but if their revival was seen as temporary they would have the unique quality of having experienced death twice. Moses and Isaiah, like Jesus, are portrayed as passing through death, resurrection and ascension, whereas Enoch and Elijah are depicted as bypassing death and experiencing only ascension without resurrection.

4

Martyrdom and resurrection in late Second Temple Judaism

In 168 BC, Antiochus IV Epiphanes, the Hellenistic king of the Seleucid dynasty who ruled over Syria and Judaea, set out to invade the rival Hellenistic Kingdom of the Ptolemies in Egypt. His plans were frustrated by the intervention of the Roman fleet, dispatched by the Senate to put an end to the expansionist plans of the Seleucids. Humiliated and compelled to retreat from Alexandria, Antiochus turned his fury on the unsympathetic Jews and after massacring the population of Jerusalem and pillaging the city, he decided to blot out the Jewish religion altogether. The Temple of Jerusalem was transformed into a sanctuary of Zeus. Every act of Jewish cult was abolished and the observance of the Law, including the commandments relating to the Sabbath and to the circumcision of boys, was prohibited (1 Mac 1:41–51; 2 Mac 6:1–2). Those Jews who refused to comply were subjected to torture, and if they resisted, they were put to death. The Second Book of the Maccabees portrays the heroic self-sacrifice of the ninety-year-old Jew Eleazar, and of seven brothers who together with their mother preferred to surrender their lives rather than transgress the Torah by eating swine flesh. Thus Jewish teachers found themselves for the first time faced with the idea of martyrdom. The new circumstances resulting from religious persecution affected the accepted attitudes concerning life and death. Commonly held wisdom maintained that the pious could expect a long and happy life. How then was one to interpret its denial by God to the eminently devout, those who went so far as to sacrifice their existence in order to remain faithful to the commandments of the Law of Moses?

The records of Jewish history of the Second Temple period testify to a twofold attempt made during the last couple of centuries of the pre-Christian era to resolve this painful dilemma, and discover a way to recompense the righteous whose life had been unjustly cut short by God. Palestinian Jews came up with the idea of bodily resurrection, while their brethren in the Greek-speaking Diaspora opted along Platonic lines for immortality of the liberated soul, enjoying divine bliss after escaping from the ephemeral and corruptible body.

The revival of individuals after their death had figurative antecedents. In the family, children succeeded parents and made life continue. On the national level the defeat and oppression inflicted on the Jewish people by their enemies and the eventual exile of Israel from their ancestral land are compared in the poetic and metaphorical language of the Old Testament prophets to striking, wounding and killing, and the divine help that followed as healing, binding and resurrection. An anticipatory example goes back to the prophet Hosea in the eighth century BC. In the shadow of the threat from Assyria, he wrote some memorable lines whose echoes continued to reverberate down to the age of the New Testament:

Come, let us return to the Lord;
For he has torn, that he may heal us;
He has stricken, and he will bind us up.

After two days, he will revive us;
On the third day he will raise us up,
That we may live before him (Hos 6:1-2).

However, the most impressive resurrection imagery comes from Ezekiel's vision of a large amount of dispersed dry bones, symbolically representing the defeated and exiled Israel, lying unburied on a plain. On God's command these bones all come together amid much rattling and are lifted up to form an enormous army:

Behold, I will cause breath to enter you,
and you shall live.
And I will lay sinews upon you,
and will cause flesh to come upon you,
and cover you with skin,
and put breath in you, and you shall live (Ezek 37:5-6).

Together with the reawakened victims of the battles, their deported compatriots who died in captivity would also be raised from their graves, and led back to the land of Israel (Ezek 37:12). The metaphor of the army of walking skeletons, shaking off the stupor of the sleep of death, offered a powerful image to the creators of the new concept of bodily resurrection. The vivified dry bones symbolized the granting of a second chance to those devout Jews who had been denied the fullness of days and the living out of their lives in peace, security and happiness.

The first attempt to apply to single individuals the symbol of collective national renaissance appears in a brief eschatological supplement inserted into the work of the eighth-century prophet Isaiah. The somewhat hazy message of chapters 24-27 probably dates to the latter part of the Persian era in the third century BC. The segment, known as the Isaiah Apocalypse, anticipates Daniel and the Second Book of the Maccabees. The author foresees that the wicked, personified by the oppressors of the Jews, are destined for perpetual annihilation:

O Lord, . . . other lords besides thee have ruled over us . . .
They are dead, they will not live; they are shades, and will not
    arise;
to that end thou hast visited them with destruction,
and wiped out all remembrance of them (Isa 26:13–14).

In contrast to the annihilation of the persecutors, corporal resurrection awaits God's dead. The persons designated as the 'dwellers in the dust' are ordered to 'awake and sing for joy' (Isa 26:19). The passage may allude to a renewed life after death awaiting the righteous. However, since the Isaiah Apocalypse represents poetry, it is possible that it speaks figuratively and refers to living people portrayed by anticipation as corpses.

The biblical Book of Daniel, which was given its final formulation in the 160s BC and is attested in manuscript fragments from Qumran dating to the end of that same century, yields the first definite expression of belief in the resurrection of the dead. The context is that of the end of times, the aftermath of the great battle between the heathen forces and the Jewish nation assisted by the angelic army of Michael, the great heavenly prince. All the chosen Jews, those whose names are inscribed in God's book, will be on the winning side. The wise and righteous teachers, resplendent in their glory like the stars of the firmament, will head the risen multitude, some of whom will inherit eternal life, while the hostile pagans and the unfaithful

Jews will be destined to everlasting shame (Dan 12:1–2). The text is usually taken as conveying the idea of corporeal resurrection, even though it does not formally assert the reunification of body and soul.

Universal resurrection, granted both to the righteous and to the wicked, foreshadows in Daniel the image of the eschatological scene adopted later by Judaism (and Christianity), in which the resuscitated dead await God's last judgement. But there is an alternative in which revival is reserved only for the just and is denied to the ungodly. This second type of scenario may be found in the Psalms of Solomon, Greek poems dating to the first century BC:

The sinner . . . fell . . . and he shall not rise up.
But they that fear the Lord shall rise to life eternal
and their life . . . shall come to an end no more (Pss of Sol.
   3:9–12)

The same concept continued to be voiced at the end of the first century AD in the Syriac Apocalypse of Baruch:

When the Messiah will return in glory to the heavens, then all who have died and set their hopes on him will rise again (2 Bar 30:1).

The idea is emphatically stressed, however, in the Second Book of the Maccabees (*c.* 100 BC), in the story of the seven brothers tortured and put to death by Antiochus Epiphanes. The brothers and their mother, who was the last to die after encouraging and witnessing the martyrdom of her sons, all professed the belief that God would recompense them with an 'everlasting renewal of life' for their sufferings and death, while the tyrant and his henchmen would be condemned to eternal destruction (2 Mac

7:1–41). The author of 2 Maccabees renders explicit the generally implicit assertion of bodily resurrection when he makes the third brother declare regarding his tongue and hands, 'I got these from Heaven, and because of [God's] laws I disdain them, and from him I hope to get them back again' (2 Mac 7:11).

These texts indicate that collective self-sacrifice in a battle fought for the sake of heaven and individual martyrdom, inflicted by the ungodly on the just as a punishment for their attachment to the Jewish religion, gave birth to the teaching of the resurrection of the dead. The doctrine, succinctly set out in the Testament of Judah – 'those who have been put to death for the Lord's sake will awake to life' (Test. of Judah 25:4) – continued to develop during the Hellenistic and Roman period, and reached its climax during the persecution of observant Jews in the course of the second war against Rome under Hadrian in AD 132–135. The rabbis of the Talmudic age went so far as to specify that a man's risen body would be exactly the same as the one he had possessed when he died: the lame would be raised lame and the blind blind, but they would be healed if found among the righteous (Eccl.R 1:4; GenR 95:1).

In addition to the idea of bodily resurrection, which was the main eschatological concept of Palestinian Judaism and of New Testament Christianity of the Pauline variety, we encounter in the Apocrypha and the rest of post-biblical Jewish literature the notion of a purely spiritual survival, usually designated as the immortality of the soul. It is important to observe that the expression 'eternal life', commonly used in the New Testament too, can equally apply to either form of survival.

The principal source of the notion of spiritual survival

is the Wisdom of Solomon, a work composed by a Jew in Greek and approximately dated between 50 BC and AD 50. Its main message is that the incorruptible souls of the righteous will enjoy eternal immortality:

God created man for incorruption
and made him in the image of his own eternity,
but through the devil's envy death entered the world,
and those who belong to his party experience it.
But the souls of the righteous are in the hand of God,
and no torment will ever touch them.
In the eyes of the foolish they seemed to have died,
and their departure was thought to be an affliction,
and their going from us to be their destruction;
but they are at peace.
For though in the sight of men they were punished,
their hope is full of immortality (Wis 2:23–3:4).

The same escape of the soul from Hades to live on for ever with God is also testified to in the wisdom sayings attributed to Pseudo-Phocylides, a Hellenized Jew writing in the first century BC:

All alike are corpses, but God rules over the souls.
Hades is our common eternal home and fatherland,
a common place for all, poor and kings.
We humans live not for a long time, but for a season.
But our soul is immortal and lives ageless for ever
(Ps.-Phoc. 111–115).

Another Hellenistic work, the Fourth Book of the Maccabees, also underlines that the righteous martyrs, who have given their lives for the Torah, share the destiny of

43

Abraham, Isaac, Jacob and all the Patriarchs. They join the choir of their fathers, having received from God 'pure and deathless souls' in exchange for their mortal coil (4 Mac 16:25; 18:23). Josephus attributes a similar view to the martyr-teachers Judas and Matthias, who were put to death by Herod for exhorting their pupils to pull down the golden eagle from the Temple. They argued that self-sacrifice for the laws of one's country was rewarded by 'immortality and an abiding sense of felicity' (*War* 1:650).

Likewise the Essene martyrs, who preferred torture and death by the hands of the Romans to the denial of their religion by cursing Moses or eating forbidden food, 'resigned their souls, confident that they would receive them back again' (*War* 2:152–153). Also Eleazar ben Yair, the captain of Masada, encouraging his men not to be taken alive by the Romans, portrays death as the act 'that gives liberty to the soul and permits it to depart to its own pure abode' (*War* 7:343).

Spiritual survival is bestowed for all eternity not only on martyrs, but also on those who have died in righteousness, according to the Book of Admonitions of the Ethiopic Enoch (chapters 91–105). The spirits of the just will live and rejoice and their memory will remain with God (1 En 103:4), and in the Parables of Enoch (chapters 37–72), the risen righteous will be 'like angels in heaven' (1 En 51:4), reminiscent of Jesus' similar saying in the New Testament (Mk 12:25; Mt 22:30; Lk 20:36).

These excerpts will give the reader a useful insight into the Jewish representation of afterlife, but the picture can be completed by the account of Enoch's visit to the realm of the dead and to Paradise, described in the First Book of Enoch, chapters 22, 25–27. The imagery differs from the common biblical idea of a subterranean underworld and locates Sheol in the western extremity of the world. Led by the angel Raphael, Enoch climbs a high mountain with huge caves where the souls of the deceased reside, separated according to their conduct in the past. A spring with bright waters refreshes the righteous while the wicked suffer. After the final judgement the ungodly, who have already received their punishment on earth, will be annihilated without trace. Those among the wicked who have escaped chastisement in their lifetime will be raised and transferred to the Valley of Hinnom (*Ge' Hinnom* = Gehenna) to suffer everlasting torment, while the righteous will inhabit the mountain of God at the summit of which stands the divine throne.

The surveyed literary evidence makes it unquestionable that the ideas of resurrection and incorporeal immortality were not unknown in Palestinian and Diaspora Jewry during the final centuries of the Second Temple. Nevertheless, before directly confronting the Gospels and Paul, three further questions need to be answered:

1. How widely and deeply did the concept of resurrection affect first-century AD Jewish society?

2. Did the Jews in the age of Jesus envisage resurrection in individual historical terms as distinct from the great eschatological event outlined in the literature of the period?

3. Is there any indication that they expected the Messiah to die and rise from the dead?

5

Jewish attitudes to afterlife in the age of Jesus

There is no doubt that the ideas of resurrection and immortality were sporadically attested in the latest layers of biblical literature as well as in the early post-biblical writings of Judaism, but does this mean that they had widely penetrated the religious consciousness of the Jews of the period? In the absence of direct reports, the best we can do is to examine the contemporaneous historical sources that describe the beliefs prevalent in that age among diverse Jewish groups. Thanks to Philo, Josephus, the Dead Sea Scrolls and the oldest strata of rabbinic literature, it is possible to arrive at an approximate assessment of the religious attitudes of the society in which Jesus ministered and to which the earliest Christian message, anchored on the notion of his resurrection, was first preached.

Let us begin with the Egyptian philosopher and religious teacher Philo of Alexandria (*c.* 20/10 BC–AD 40/50), the quintessential representative, indeed the personification, of a fully Hellenized Jew. He professed a Greek-type doctrine of immortality. For him, the soul was incarcerated in the body during a man's life. It was 'like a prisoner in the gaol', but on death it retrieved its freedom. 'When it has gone out of this city', Philo remarks, 'its thought and reflections are at liberty, like the hands and feet of the unbound prisoner' (*On Drunkenness* 101). Even more strikingly, echoing Plato's pun, Philo equates the body (*sôma*) with a tomb (*sêma*), out of which the soul arises for true life.

When we are living, the soul is dead and has been entombed in the body as a sepulchre; whereas should we die, the soul lives forthwith its own proper life, and is released from the body, the baneful corpse to which it was tied (Allegory 108).

It should surprise no one that the notion of the resurrection of the body never appears in his vast work. For educated Hellenists, reunion of the noble and liberated soul with the vile body was a denial of the highest philosophical principles, as St Paul had to find out for himself when he engaged in debate with learned Hellenes at 'speakers' corner' in Athens (Acts 17:16–33). It would seem, therefore, that the Christian preaching focused on the cross and resurrection of Christ appealed only to uncultured Greeks. Indeed, among Paul's habitual Greek clientele 'not many . . . were wise according to worldly standards' (1 Cor 1:26).

In a similar fashion, the upper echelons of Palestinian Jewish society also appear to have been hostile to the idea of resurrection. The leading classes of the Jerusalem priesthood and their wealthy and well-schooled aristocratic allies, who together formed the party of the Sadducees, were basically traditionalists. They did not speculate overmuch about afterlife and stuck to the conventional biblical wisdom emphatically and fatalistically defined in the Apocrypha by the author of the Book of Ecclesiasticus, Jesus Ben Sira, himself probably a priest from Jerusalem:

Do not fear the sentence of death;
Remember your former days and the end of life;

This is the decree from the Lord for all flesh,
And how can you reject the good pleasure of the Most High?
Whether life is for ten, or a hundred or a thousand years,
There is no inquiry about it in Hades (Ecclus 41:3–4).

According to Josephus, himself of chief-priestly origin (although at the age of nineteen he decided to switch his allegiance to the Pharisees (*Life* 1–12)), the Sadducees rejected the idea of survival after death and did not believe in future retribution. In Josephus' own words, 'The Sadducees hold that the soul perishes along with the body' (*Ant* 18:16), that is to say, at death life is extinguished for good. He further declares, 'As for the persistence of the soul after death, penalties in the underworld, and rewards, they [the Sadducees] will have none of them' (*War* 2:165). In the Gospels the Sadducee creed proclaims, 'There is no resurrection' (Mk 12:18; Mt 22:23; Lk 20:27). In a polemical episode, to be examined later (pp. 69–72), the Sadducees ridicule the notion of rising from the dead (Mk 12:18–27; Mt 22:23–32; Lk 20:27–38).

The Acts of the Apostles goes even further than Josephus and the Gospels when it turns the Sadducees into complete materialists who denied not only the resurrection of the dead, but also the existence of angels and spirits (Acts 23:8). However, this exaggeration should probably be blamed more on the Gentile Luke's unfamiliarity with Palestinian Jewish thought than on the Sadducees, for angels are commonly mentioned in the Bible and the Sadducees were sticklers for the letter of scripture.

The stand taken by the Essenes on resurrection is more difficult to establish. Josephus, who claims to have experienced the life of this sect and studied their philosophy (*Life* 10), reports that the kind of afterlife they envisaged was different from resurrection. His final word on the subject in *Jewish Antiquities* (end of the first century AD) was that the Essenes believed in spiritual survival, the immortality of the soul (*Ant* 18:18). In the earlier account of the *Jewish War*, Josephus, like Philo and Hellenistic Judaism, paints a detailed Platonic canvas that after death incorruptible souls receive eternal reward or punishment.

For it is a fixed belief of theirs that the body is corruptible and its constituent matter impermanent, but that the soul is immortal and imperishable. Emanating from the finest ether, these souls become entangled, as it were, in the prison-house of the body, to which they are dragged down by a sort of natural spell; but when once they are released from the bonds of the flesh, then, as though liberated from a long servitude, they rejoice and are borne aloft. Sharing the belief of the sons of Greece, they maintain that for the virtuous souls there is reserved an abode beyond the ocean, a place which is not oppressed by rain or snow or heat, but is refreshed by the ever gentle breath of the west wind coming in from the ocean; while they relegate base souls to a murky and tempestuous dungeon, big with never-ending punishment ... Their aim was first to establish the doctrine of the immortality of the soul, and secondly to promote virtue and to deter from vice; for the good are made better in their lifetime by the hope of a reward after death, and the passions of the wicked are restrained by the fear that, even though they escape detection while alive, they will undergo neverending punishment after their decease (War 2:154–157).

If this was a true picture of the Essene representation of afterlife, a message centred on a risen Messiah (like the Jesus preached by Christians) would not have had much hope of success among them. However, for whatever it's worth, the Church father Hippolytus has left us a second version, purported to be Josephus' account, in which a very different picture is sketched:

The doctrine of the resurrection also is firmly held among them. For they confess that the flesh also will rise and be immortal as the soul is already immortal, which they now say, when separated from the body, enters a place of fragrant air and light, to rest until the judgement . . . (Refutation of All the Heresies 9:27).

Is the difference due to the pen of Hippolytus, wishing to portray the Essenes as proto-Christians, or was Josephus guilty of twisting the evidence in order to make the Essene teaching palatable to his Greek readers? While the first view is more commonly held, there are defenders of the second, too. Clarification of the problem may be sought by means of the Dead Sea Scrolls.

However, the outcome of the study of the Qumran texts both on the subject of afterlife in general, and on resurrection in particular, is rather disappointing. The Scrolls contain a surprisingly small amount of relevant information. There are some general allusions to afterlife which may coincide with Josephus' idea of spiritual immortality. For example, the Sons of Light are promised 'eternal joy in life without end, a crown of glory and a garment of majesty in light without end' (1QS 4:7–8). They are also said to share their future destiny with angels called the Holy Ones and the Sons of Heaven (1QS 11:5–9). A couple of poetic passages may be interpreted as referring to bodily resurrection. Thus people who 'lie in the dust' and 'bodies gnawed by worms' are commanded to hoist a banner or rise from the dust to the counsel of God's truth (1QH 14:34–35; 19:12). Nevertheless, it is equally possible that the language is allegorical and no actual bodily revival is envisaged. The only text among the hundreds of manuscripts found at Qumran which clearly refers to resurrection is the so-called Messianic Apocalypse, a verse composition that includes a line from Isaiah (61:1), to which is added a reference to the resurrection of the dead, namely that God will 'heal the wounded and revive the dead and bring good news to the poor' (4Q521, frag. 2 ii, line 12). The statement could possibly signify that the Qumran community believed in the rising of the dead, but since the manuscript exhibits no sectarian features, it may not belong to the Essenes and could represent a work akin to late biblical poetry such as Isaiah 24–27.

All in all, the available evidence does not permit us to conclude that either the Essenes, as portrayed by Josephus, or the Qumran sectaries of the Scrolls, were champions of the belief in bodily resurrection, although there is evidence that both of them contemplated an afterlife in the form of the immortality of the soul. As for Philo's notices on the Essenes, they have nothing to say on the subject.

This leaves us only with the Pharisees, who were the renowned protagonists of the doctrine of the resurrection. Josephus reports their teaching in each of his three works, the *War*, *Against Apion* and the *Antiquities*, and on a further occasion in the *War* he expresses in a speech his own Pharisaic convictions about afterlife.

His doctrine on the resurrection is not entirely homogeneous, nor does it clearly convey the teaching of mainstream Pharisaism. In his earliest summary, he brings into relief the incorruptibility of the spirit of man, but his description of the spirit's reunion with the body sounds more like metempsychosis or transmigration of the soul than bodily resurrection. He also appears to restrict corporeal revival to the righteous, as did 2 Maccabees and the

Psalms of Solomon before him (see p. 41). The pious alone are to enjoy eternal corporeal bliss, while the wicked souls, seemingly without new bodies, are to suffer everlasting torment: 'Every soul, they maintain, is imperishable, but the soul of the good alone passes into another body, while the souls of the wicked suffer eternal punishment' (*War* 2:163).

In the same *Jewish War*, in an effort to dissuade his fellow rebels from committing suicide, Josephus assures them that taking their own lives will deprive them of new bodies in God's realm:

Know you not that they who depart this life in accordance with the law of nature and repay the loan which they received from God, when He who lent is pleased to reclaim it, win eternal renown; that their houses and families are secure; that their souls, remaining spotless and obedient, are allotted the most holy place in heaven, whence, in the revolution of the ages, they return to find in chaste bodies a new habitation? But as for those who have laid mad hands upon themselves, the darker regions of the nether world receive their souls . . . (*War* 3:374–375).

Even in his two later works, *Against Apion* and *Jewish Antiquities*, written in the AD 90s, he seems to grant the privilege of resurrection only to the good; the ungodly are condemned to remain eternally imprisoned in Sheol:

They believe that the souls have power to survive death and that there are rewards and punishments under the earth for those who have led lives of virtue or vice: eternal imprisonment is the lot of evil souls, while the good souls receive an easy passage to a new life (Ant 18:14).

In *Against Apion* Josephus insists that only the strict observers of the Law, and especially those who are ready to die rather than disobey the commandments, will reap the reward of the resurrection:

For those ... who live in accordance with our laws the prize is not silver and gold, no crown of wild olive or of parsley with any such public mark of distinction. No; each individual, relying on the witness of his own conscience, and the lawgiver's prophecy, confirmed by the sure testimony of God, is firmly persuaded that to those who observe the laws, and, if they must needs die for them, willingly meet death, God has granted a renewed existence and in the revolution of the ages the gift of a better life (c. Ap. 2:217–18).

Shortly after the time of Josephus, around the turn of the first century AD, the rabbinic heirs of the Pharisees continued to propound, without distinguishing between the good and the bad, the doctrine of resurrection as one of the two pivotal teachings of Judaism, the other being the divine origin of the Torah. Thus the tractate Sanhedrin of the Mishnah, the oldest rabbinic code of law, declares:

All Israelites have a share in the world to come ... And these are they who have no share in the world to come: he that says that there is no resurrection of the dead [prescribed in the Law], and that the Law is not from Heaven (mSanh 10:1).[1]

At about the same time (c. AD 100) was formulated also the second benediction of the *Tephillah* (the Prayer par excellence), also bearing the title of the *Eighteen Benedictions*, recited in standing position three times a day, morning, afternoon and evening, as specific thanksgiving to God for raising the dead. It has been preserved in two versions, the

Babylonian and the Palestinian, but on this point both convey the same message:

Lord, Thou art almighty for ever, who makest the dead alive . . . Thou makest the dead alive out of great mercy . . . Thou keepest thy word faithfully to them who sleep in the dust . . . Thou art faithful to make the dead alive. Blessed art Thou, Lord, who makest the dead alive (Babylonian version).

Thou art mighty . . . Thou livest for ever and raisest the dead . . . Thou providest for the living and makest the dead alive . . . Blessed art Thou, Lord, who makest the dead alive (Palestinian version).

It would seem, therefore, that by the second century AD, faith in bodily resurrection was an essential constituent of the Pharisaic-rabbinic religion. But at first sight there is no positive evidence to indicate that this was the case during the lifetime of Jesus, the ministry of Paul or the early decades of Christianity. Yet for the evaluation of how prepared the audiences of Jesus and of the apostolic preachers were for the idea of the resurrection, it would be useful to have the means to grasp the extent of the spread of this notion in the various layers of Jewish and Graeco-Roman society in the first century AD.

To begin with, the three groups, Sadducees, Essenes and Pharisees, about whose attitude towards resurrection we know something, represent only a small fraction of the Jewish population of Palestine in the age of Jesus.

No source supplies direct information about the number of the Sadducees, who comprised the upper layers of the priesthood and their aristocratic lay supporters, but attempts have been made to estimate the size of the Temple personnel, priests and Levites. Already about four hundred years before the age of Jesus the Book of Nehemiah refers to 1,192 priests in Jerusalem (Neh 11:10–19). Closer to New Testament times, towards the end of the second century BC, the author of the Letter of Aristeas asserted that seven hundred priests were on duty every day in the Temple, not counting those in charge of sacrifices (Aristeas 95). Since the service in the sanctuary was performed by one of the 24 weekly units, or 'courses', each of which was on duty twice a year, 24 × say 750 would give a total for the Jewish clergy (priests and Levites) of eighteen thousand. In the late first century AD Josephus suggests a similar figure when he speaks of four priestly tribes, each comprising upwards of five thousand men, amounting to over twenty thousand (c. AP. 21:108). While it is known that by that time some of the priests adhered to the teaching of the Pharisees, one can still suppose that a fair proportion of them held to the party doctrine laid down by the upper clergy, and were opposed to the idea of resurrection.

As for the membership of the Pharisee associations, we know from Josephus that, as a body, over six thousand of them refused to swear the oath of allegiance to Herod the Great (*Ant* 17:42). The number of the Essenes was put both by Philo (*Omnis probus* 75) and by Josephus (*Ant* 18:20) at above four thousand.

What do these figures tell us? Among those who did not believe in the resurrection of the dead we may count more than four thousand Essenes and probably a good proportion of the 15,000–20,000-strong Temple staff, together no doubt with their families and their upper-class lay allies. Against these stood some six thousand Pharisees, their families and followers. Taken together, both the opponents and the supporters of the doctrine of the resurrection formed only a small portion of the Jewish population of

Palestine in the first century AD, estimated at between 500,000 and 1,000,000, but more likely to have amounted to between 500,000 and 600,000.[2] It is widely maintained, however, that the Pharisees controlled most of the Jewish population of Roman Palestine, and that consequently the majority of the Jews of the Holy Land believed in the resurrection of the dead. It has even been proposed that the fairly widespread, though far from universally adopted custom of secondary burial, *viz.* the collecting of the bones of the deceased and placing them in ossuaries, was a Pharisee innovation inspired by faith in individual revival. But this is a misunderstanding that must be dispelled.

In truth, the thesis of an all-pervasive Pharisaic impact on the whole Jewish population has no evidential support. According to Josephus, the Pharisees were influential, not across the board of society, but mostly among the 'townsfolk' or the 'inhabitants of the cities' (*Ant* 18:15), that is to say, their followers were recruited among the moderately well-to-do urban artisan classes. Also, territorially, their main constituency was Jerusalem and the towns of Judaea.

But Judaea differed from Galilee, and in this connection one should recall that in the age of Jesus, Pharisee presence in Galilee was scarce, if it existed at all. It became dominant only after the resettlement of the defeated Judaeans in the northern province following the first rebellion against Rome (AD 66–70). A careful reader of the New Testament will observe that various Pharisees and scribes, mentioned in the Gospels, are explicitly said to have been visitors from Jerusalem and not Galilean citizens (Mk 3:22; 7:1; Mt 12:24; 15:1). The impression given by Mark and Matthew of a Pharisee-free Galilee is further reinforced by Josephus. He refers to the presence of only three Pharisees during his tenure as revolutionary military commander of the province, and names them as Jonathan, Ananias and Jozar. But they were not local people. They were sent to the northern province by the chief Pharisee of the capital, Simeon ben Gamaliel, to engineer the downfall of Josephus (*Life* 197).

As far as the general influence of Pharisaic ideas was concerned, one should further remember that in both Judaea and Galilee the bulk of the population did not reside in cities, the Pharisees' strongholds, but lived in the country. They were the village farmers and agricultural workers, the 'people of the land' (*'am ha-arets*), who ploughed the fields and cultivated the orchards, olive groves and vineyards, as appears so clearly in the rural parables of Jesus. So it would seem that we simply do not know how generally accepted the doctrinal leadership of the Pharisees was in first-century AD Palestine, and consequently how widespread the belief in bodily resurrection was at that time.[3]

If literature provides no further assistance for an assessment of the impact of the Pharisaic belief in resurrection in wider Jewish society, can archaeology and funeral inscriptions help? Some experts have voiced a firmly negative opinion. In his monumental study of the Essene doctrine on life after death, Émile Puech declares that funerary art on tombstones and ossuaries displays no clear hint at eschatological expectations.[4] The author of the latest monograph on funeral epigraphy, P. W. van der Horst, also complains of the 'disappointingly little information' the inscriptions yield about life after death.[5] Such pessimistic forecasts must not, however, prevent us from re-examining the evidence.

The most common decorative figure on Jewish ossuaries

and tombstones is the *menorah*, the seven-branched lamp-stand. Modelled on the candelabrum of the Jerusalem Temple, taken to Rome by Titus after the fall of Jerusalem, and represented on his triumphal arch constructed in the Roman Forum in AD 81, it had become the principal symbol of Judaism. Sometimes accompanied by other decorative motives, the citron (*ethrog*), the palm-branch (*lulab*) and the scroll of the Law, it appears fairly frequently on Jewish tombs and bone boxes. There is no unanimity regarding its meaning. It can merely denote the Jewishness of the person or possibly his priestly connections. E. R. Goodenough, the leading expert on the subject, remarks however that the *menorah* was of the greatest importance for Jews to have on their tombstones and symbolized yearning for light in the darkness of the grave.[6] It appears fairly often in the Jewish catacombs of Rome and in Beth Shearim, dating to the third and fourth centuries AD, but there are also a few earlier attestations. The oldest is on what is known as Jason's tomb in Jerusalem, but what in fact is the tomb of the priestly family of the Sons of Hezir (second or first century BC). Two more figure on Palestinian ossuaries,[7] probably belonging to the first or second century AD. A few representations of the *menorah* may be found on Egyptian Jewish tombs, probably from the second century AD. Nothing directly connects the candelabrum with the resurrection of the dead, but there is a legitimate surmise that this symbol of illumination is meant to remind the onlooker of a bright and hopeful hereafter of some sort.

Only a small proportion of the funeral inscriptions allude to the beliefs of the deceased or of those who ordered the epitaphs. On one ossuary the idea of resurrection is firmly rejected in the Sadducee manner: 'No man goes up [from the grave]; not Eleazar or Sapphira' (Rahmani, no. 455). Unparalleled is the invitation tainted with irony that the Roman Jew, Leo Leontius, has issued to his associates: 'Friends, I am waiting for you here' (*Amici ego vos hic exspecto*) (CIJ *32).[8] Another inscription from Beth Shearim, 'Good luck with your resurrection', may be either cynical or a serious affirmation of belief in the reawakening of the dead (BS II, 194). As for the often repeated 'No one is immortal', a phrase that is found on pagan epitaphs as well, it expresses the outlook of the Old Testament and the Sadducees, although some detect a hopeful overtone in the exhortation, 'Be of good courage!' (BS II, 59, 127, 136, etc.) placed before it. 'May your sleep be peaceful!', frequently read on Roman epitaphs, can also be interpreted as a wish for undisturbed rest in the tomb and a protection against grave robbers on whom God's judgement accompanied by a curse is again and again invoked. However, the word 'peace', sometimes written as *shalom* in Hebrew, is capable of deeper meaning, implying fullness and religious perfection.

A small number of Greek inscriptions from Leontopolis in Egypt and Beth Shearim seem to allude to the idea of immortality. The soul of Arsinoe, a young Jewess who died in labour when she was producing her first child, 'has gone to the holy ones', we read on an inscription dating to the twenty-fifth year of Augustus or 5 BC (CIJ 1510). Rachel, aged about thirty years, entertains a good hope in God's mercy, which implies expectation of some form of future life (CIJ 1513), and in a Hebrew inscription from Antino-opolis a Jew called Lazar expects his soul to find rest in the 'bundle of the living' (CIJ 1534). In a similar Greek epitaph from Beth Shearim someone wishes that the souls of his or her parents 'be bound in the bundle of immortal life' (BS II, 130), while a certain Hesechios, also from Beth Shearim, threatens with the loss of 'a portion in eternal life' anyone daring to open his and his wife's grave (BS II, 129). Karteria and Zenobia, her daughter who arranged her funeral, long to 'enjoy again new indestructible riches' (BS II, 183). In these inscriptions the spiritual survival of Hellenistic Judaism is voiced without any hint at the doctrine characteristic of the Pharisees.

The very common wish at Beth Shearim that the deceased should 'possess a good portion' (*eumoirei, eumoros*), a Greek phrase reminiscent of the Hebrew Pharisaic-rabbinic 'portion' (*ḥeleq*) in the world to come, may insinuate the idea of resurrection, but it could also refer only to the survival of the soul. Indeed, a clear confession of belief in bodily revivification is exceptional among the epitaphs. I have counted two or possibly three occurrences in the Corpus of Jewish Inscriptions, the Palestinian ossuaries and the Beth Shearim material. The uncertain case, already referred to, is 'Good luck with your resurrection' (BS II, 194). If it is taken at its face value with no undertone of cynicism, it has a positive religious significance. By the way, this is the only case where the term *anastasis* (rising, resurrection) is used. Of the other two, the first comes from Beth Shearim, and employs the verb 'to revive', while issuing a warning against interference with the contents of the grave. 'Anyone who changes this lady's place, He who promised to revive (*zôpoiêse*) the dead will Himself judge [him]' (BS II, 162). The second, a direct proclamation of faith in the resurrection of the dead, is the versified Latin epitaph of the Roman Jewess, Regina. It was set up in the second century AD by her husband, with whom she lived twenty-one years, four months and eight days:

Hic Regina sita est tali contecta sepulcro
Quod coniunx statuit respondens eius amori . . .
Rursum victura reditura ad lumina rursum
Nam sperare potest ideo quod surgat in aevum
Promissum quae vera fides dignisque piisque
Quae meruit sedem venerandi ruris habere
(CIJ 476).

Here lies Regina, concealed in such a sepulcher
That her husband has set up responding to her love . . .
She will live again and will again return to the light
For she can hope to rise for eternity
As is promised by true faith to the worthy and the pious.
She has deserved to have a place in the venerable land.

The expression *surgere in aevum* (to rise for eternity) definitely refers to corporeal resurrection and if the phrase 'venerable land' denotes the Holy Land, the writer of the poem seems to allude to the rabbinic idea that the resurrection of the dead will take place, or at least will begin, in Jerusalem.

In conclusion, let us revert to the first question posed at the end of the previous chapter: How widely and deeply did the concept of resurrection affect first-century AD Jewish society? The long and the short of the answer is that the notion of bodily resurrection propagated by the Pharisees was alien to first-century Hellenistic Jews, and was on the whole unfamiliar in most layers of Palestinian Jewry. Our study of the New Testament will have to keep this remark firmly in mind.

II

Resurrection and eternal life in the New Testament

6

Introductory note

Our survey of the Hebrew Bible, post-biblical Second
Temple literature and archaeology has shown that the idea
of the resurrection of the dead was a latecomer in Jewish
religious thought. Moreover, it turned out to be only one
of the possibilities of man's survival after death. Since the
individuality of the deceased was thought to continue even
beyond the grave, as the story of the reappearance of
the prophet Samuel in the Bible indicates, the just and the
wicked, originally thought to share the same address in the
underworld, ended up being moved to different domains.
The righteous Jews kept company with the holy Patriarchs,
while the ungodly were to suffer the torments of hell.

With the emergence of the idea of an eschatological
divine judgement inaugurating the kingdom of God,
the ultimate reward of the good and chastisement of the
wicked were substituted for the unilateral notion of recompense, whether resurrection or immortality, awarded
only to the pious. This type of resurrection, as distinguished from resuscitation shortly after death, like the acts
performed by Elijah and Elisha, was conceived as a peculiar
occurrence marking the end of times. Finally, however
significant resurrection appeared to be to the eschatologically motivated, it occupied only a small area of the broad
religious canvas of late Second Temple Judaism.

The New Testament completely altered the vista and changed the perspective. In it the individual resurrection of one Jew, Jesus of Nazareth, predominates. It is set in time and space and integrated into history, and is anticipated by other resurrections achieved by or connected with him. The rising of Jesus is claimed to account for the religious movement, later designated as Christianity, that two thousand years on is still flourishing and numbers among its adherents a substantial portion of mankind. According to the Gospels, Jesus had repeatedly prepared his intimates for his return from the tomb yet it hit them suddenly like a bolt out of the blue.

The situation is profoundly perplexing and the historian must come to grips with this puzzle. In the first instance, he has to re-examine the written evidence. What do the accounts of the burial and resurrection of Jesus actually say? How do the four Gospel narratives relate to one another? How do they fit into the eschatological teaching of Jesus about eternal life and resurrection? How should one judge Jesus' predictions of his rising from the dead and the claim made by him and/or his immediate followers that the resurrection was the fulfilment of biblical prophecies? Finally, since the chapters relative to the resurrection form only a small part of the Gospels – eight verses in Mark, twenty in Matthew, fifty-three in Luke and fifty-six in John – how did they manage to take on such an overall importance?

To approach all these questions in the right order, we shall first examine the teaching of Jesus on resurrection and eternal life (chapter 7). This will be followed by a survey of the passages in the New Testament where Jesus predicts his rising from the dead, or claims that the event has been foretold by the biblical prophets (chapter 8). The next step will take us to the resurrection narratives, first the accounts of Jesus raising other people from the dead (chapter 9) and above all, the records of his own resurrection (chapter 10) which will then be fully analyzed and initially evaluated (chapter 11). The discussion of the resurrection of Jesus will be followed by its interpretation in the Acts of the Apostles (chapter 12), St Paul (chapter 13) and the remaining writings of the New Testament (chapter 14). The full survey will permit us to investigate the meaning of the resurrection in its Jewish and Graeco-Roman context (chapter 15) with a glance at its overall significance in antiquity and in the twenty-first century.

7

The teaching of Jesus on resurrection and eternal life

1. Resurrection

Ever since St Paul wrote his letters in the fifties AD, the resurrection of Jesus and resurrection in general have stood at the centre of New Testament thought and Christian theology. Paul is adamant on the subject: without belief in resurrection, primarily in the resurrection of Christ, his preaching is baseless, the Christians are misled by him and their faith is futile (1 Cor 15:12–17). In these circumstances one would justifiably expect to find in the teaching of Jesus, as handed down in the Gospels, numerous references to the raising of the dead and to his own resurrection. Those who labour under such an illusion must brace themselves for a big surprise. General pronouncements by Jesus on resurrection are few and far between. Allusions to his rising can be counted on the fingers of one hand, and when scrutinized with critical eyes, they turn out to be inauthentic. Let us investigate these passages, leaving to chapters 9 and 10 the examination of the narrative accounts: the 'resurrection miracles' performed by Jesus and the Gospel stories of his own resurrection.

There are two passages in the Synoptic Gospels dealing with resurrection in which Jesus is neither the resuscitator nor the raised (see chapter 9), and four predictions are recorded concerning his own rising (see chapter 8). Out of the two general resurrection references, one is merely cursory and simply dates another event; the other is substantive, and is embedded in a controversy story. The former occurs in a parable dealing with the guests summoned to a banquet which is preserved only in Luke (Lk 14:7−14). In it, Jesus advises the host to show disinterested benevolence by inviting not friends, members of his family and *rich* neighbours, but 'the poor, the maimed, the lame and the blind'; those who are unable to reciprocate his generosity. So, instead of hoping for immediate repayment in the form of similar invitations to festivities, he postpones his reward until the end, until 'the resurrection of the just' (Lk 14:14).

There is only one relatively extensive Synoptic treatment of the problem of the resurrection ascribed to Jesus. It appears in a debate with the Sadducees in a collection of controversies situated in Jerusalem. However, while the other polemics on divorce, the authority of Jesus, the legitimacy of the payment of taxes to Rome and the precise identity of the Son of David fit well into the context of Jesus' arrival in the Holy City during the week of the fateful Passover, the meeting with the Sadducees is haphazard. It is no doubt put in its present place because it is a doctrinal argument which must have taken place in the Holy City, and in the Synoptic Gospels Jesus only once visits the capital of Judaea.

*And Sadducees came to him, who say that there is no resurrection;
and they asked him a question, saying, 'Teacher, Moses wrote for us
that if a man's brother dies and leaves a wife, but leaves no child,
the man must take the wife, and raise up children for his brother.
There were seven brothers; the first took a wife, and when he died
left no children; and the second took her, and died, leaving no children;
and the third likewise; and the seven left no children. Last of all the
woman also died. In the resurrection whose wife will she be? For the
seven had her as wife'* (Mk, Mt, Lk). *Jesus said to them, Is not this
why you are wrong, that you know neither the scriptures nor the
power of God?*

*For when they rise from the dead, they neither marry nor are given
in marriage, but are* **like the angels in heaven** (Mk, Mt).

[The sons of this age marry and are given in marriage;
but those who are worthy to attain to that age and to the
resurrection from the dead neither marry, nor are given in
marriage, for they cannot die any more, because they are
**equal to angels, and are sons of God, being sons of
the resurrection** (Lk).]

The anecdote, which carries the message on resurrection, recounts the curious adventure of a Jewish woman,
told against the background of the biblical law regulating
leviratic marriage (Deut 25:5–6). The Mosaic legislation
obliged a childless widow to marry her deceased husband's
brother if he was willing to take her as his wife. The purpose of the rule was to provide the former husband with
an heir: the first male child born of the new union was
indeed legally recognized as the deceased brother's son.

In the story quoted by the Sadducees, the woman went
through successive marriages with her six brothers-in-law,

burying them all one after the other, without producing a child. Finally she also joined the seven dead husbands in Sheol. The tantalizing question put to Jesus concerned the eschatological future of the widow of seven spouses: 'In the resurrection whose wife will she be?'

Most critical commentators rightly assume that the conflict is inauthentic and probably reflects by anticipation arguments opposing the haughty Sadducees and the representatives of the apostolic Church in the latter part of the first century, but there is no reason to doubt that the ideas expressed here correspond to the eschatological thought of Jesus.

The tale itself smacks of fiction. From what we learn from other Gospel accounts about Jesus as polemist – for instance his proud refusal to declare to the envoys of the chief priests the source of his authority (see Mk 11:27–33; Mt 21:23–27; Lk 20:1–8) – it is hard to imagine him naively putting up with what seems to be a cynical leg pull by the Sadducees. The Gospel story has all the appearances of an upper-class Jews' joke, addressed not to Jesus whom the chief priests feared, but to the apostles who for them counted as uncouth boors from Galilee (see Acts 4:13).

The reply placed on Jesus' lips provides an insight into how some first-century AD Jews, and possibly Jesus himself, conceived of the state of a person raised from the dead. The 'sons of the resurrection' were thought to be *bodiless* and resembled the 'angels of God' or the 'sons of God'. The picture is paralleled in contemporaneous Jewish literature such as the First Book of Enoch (in the section of the Parables, datable to the last quarter of the first century AD), whose author, like Jesus of the Synoptics, compared the resurrected righteous to the 'angels in heaven' (1 En 51:4). The Second Book of Baruch (equally from the late first century AD) also speaks of the glory of the risen just that is similar to, and even surpasses, the splendour of the angels (2 Bar 51:5, 10, 12). So for Jesus, or at least for his later disciples, the sons of the resurrection had an angelic, non-corporeal, quality. If so, the idea of marriage, with its bodily implications, was inapplicable to them.

Consequently, in the eyes of Jesus, resurrected persons, or more precisely the raised just, the people he seems to have most of the time envisaged as worthy of resurrection, were purely bodiless beings without the needs and functions of flesh and blood.[1] This would imply that in Jesus' mind the distinction between resurrection and mere spiritual survival was minimal. Study of his concept of 'life' or 'eternal life' will confirm this conclusion (see pp. 75–8). The only sustainable conclusion is that corporeal resurrection played no significant part in the thinking of Jesus although he was undoubtedly aware of the idea. If so, the concept must have gained popularity at a later stage.

i. Resurrection in the Gospel of John

By contrast, due to the peculiar perspective of the evangelist, a totally different picture emerges from the Gospel of John. John's Jesus pre-existed in heaven. He descended to earth for a short duration and he had long since reascended to heaven to be with the Father by the time the Gospel was written at the turn of the first century AD. Some of his followers were already dead and others were expected to die before the D-day of the final resurrection. In John's eyes, the principal task Jesus, the glorified Son of God, received from the Father was the raising of the dead, or more specifically the raising of his deceased disciples on the last day, as is obvious from the words placed by the evangelist on Jesus' lips:

*For I have come down from heaven, not to do my own will, but the will of him who sent me; and this is the will of him who sent me, that I should lose nothing of all that he has given me, but **raise** it up at the last day. For this is the will of my Father, that everyone who sees the Son and believes in him should have **eternal life**; and I will **raise** him up on the last day* (Jn 6:38–40).

*No one can come to me unless the Father who sent me draws him; and I will **raise** him up at the last day* (Jn 6:44).

The means by which the faithful are to be revived for ever is the symbolical body and blood of Jesus that they must sacramentally consume.

*He who eats my flesh and drinks my blood has **eternal life**, and I will **raise** him up on the last day* (Jn 6:54).

This cannibalistic allegory is hardly attributable to Jesus speaking to his Galilean listeners. Most first-century AD Palestinian Jews, hearing these words, would have been overcome by nausea. The eating of blood was a deeply ingrained biblical taboo, since the Mosaic law identified blood with life and life belongs to God alone (Lev 17:10–11). It follows, therefore, that John's words are those of a possibly Gentile Christian preacher addressed to a non-Jewish audience. Let it be recalled that even some twenty years after the death of Jesus, the council of the apostles in Jerusalem compelled non-Jews wishing to join the Church to abstain from blood (Acts 15:20), that is to say, to eat only the meat of animals slaughtered according to Jewish ritual law.

John's Jesus metaphorically presents himself to the sister of his deceased friend Lazarus as the embodiment of resurrection as far as the dead are concerned, and as the source of life for the living: 'I am the **resurrection** and the **life**; he who believes in me, though he die, yet shall he live, and whoever lives and believes in me, shall never die' (Jn 11:25).

Following the model adopted with a single exception by the Synoptics (see p. 155, n. 1, to chapter 7), in John, too, as a rule resurrection is promised to the just alone; the fate of the wicked is left out of consideration. Universal renascence of the dead – both good and evil, preceding judgement – is first mooted in the Book of Daniel before becoming common doctrine professed by rabbinic Judaism, and is heard only on a single occasion in John.

For as the Father has life in himself, so he has granted the Son to have life in himself, and has given him authority to execute judgement, because he is the Son of man. Do not marvel at this; for the hour is coming when all who are in the tombs will hear his voice and come forth, those who have done good, to the **resurrection of life***, and those who have done evil, to the* **resurrection of judgement** (Jn 5:26–29).

Here ends our extremely meagre harvest of sayings on resurrection, using the actual words 'to rise' and 'resurrection', attributed to Jesus by the Gospels. However, it is possible to cast the net wider and hunt also for references to 'life' or 'eternal life', not necessarily including the concept of corporeal reawakening, in an attempt to establish whether it alters the picture.

2. Eternal life

Here again the first fact that strikes the observer is the paucity of attestation in the Synoptics; four units if parallel passages are not counted separately, as against three for resurrection.

i. The Synoptic Gospels

Although the concepts of eternal life and resurrection are interconnected, curiously they do not figure together in the Synoptic Gospels as they do in the later work of John. Nevertheless, there is one example in the Synoptics in which the idea (though not the actual term) of bodily resurrection is presumed.

And if your hand causes you to sin, cut it off; it is better for you to enter **life** *maimed than with two hands to go to hell, to the unquenchable fire. And if your foot causes you to sin, cut it off; it is better for you to enter life lame than with two feet to be thrown into hell. And if your eye causes you to sin, pluck it out; it is better for you to enter the* **kingdom of God** *[Mt: life] with one eye than with two eyes to be thrown into hell, where their worm does not die, and the fire is not quenched* (Mk 9:43–48; Mt 18:8–9).

According to Jesus, it is worth sacrificing a limb or an eye if it opens the gate to life, that is to say to eternal blessedness. Elsewhere he hyperbolically recommends self-castration if it is required for access to the kingdom of heaven (Mt 19:12).

In the other Synoptic passages, eternal life is used as the equivalent of 'kingdom of God', the central topic of the preaching of Jesus in Mark, Matthew and Luke, that plays practically no part in the Fourth Gospel. Neither formula is ever properly defined, but both indicate in general terms the transformation of the conditions of existence from those that prevail in the present era to the state of affairs in the world to come. By contrast, damnation is depicted with the help of the biblical imagery of worms and hell-fire.[2] Jesus seems less interested in the details of the future life than in the overall qualifications which authorize entry to the kingdom of God. The best illustration is yielded by the story recounting a conversation between Jesus and a pious wealthy man:

And as he was setting out on his journey, a man ran up and knelt before him, and asked him, 'Good Teacher, what must I do to inherit **eternal life***?' . . . You know the commandments . . .' And he said to [Jesus]: 'Teacher, all these I have observed from my youth.' And Jesus . . . said to him, '. . . [S]ell what you have, and give it to the poor . . .' And Jesus . . . said to his disciples, 'How hard it will be for those who have riches to enter the* **kingdom of God***! . . . It is easier for a camel to go through the eye of a needle than for a rich man to enter the* **kingdom of God***'* (Mk 10:17–25; Mt 19:16–24; Lk 18:18–25).

'Truly, I say to you, there is no one who has left their house Lk: *or wife] or brothers or sisters or mother or father or children or lands, for my sake and for* **the gospel** *[Mt:* **for my name's sake***; Lk:* **for the sake of the kingdom of God***], who will not receive a hundredfold now in this time, houses and brothers and sisters and mothers and children and lands, . . . and* **in the age to come eternal life***'* (Mk 10:29–30; Mt 19:29; Lk 18:29–30).

In his answer to the question of how to be saved, Jesus declared that obedience to God's commandments, especially as they are expressed in the Decalogue, is the way to 'eternal life', but renunciation of worldly goods, too, constitutes a simple and safe access. Indeed, approach to the kingdom of God or eternal life is hindered by wealth, and to attain it is just as impossible for a rich man as it is for a camel to pass through the eye of a needle.[3] In short, the accent is laid not on the ultimate target, but existentially, as is often the case with Jesus, on the means enabling one to reach the goal.

The typical exaggeration of abandoning parents, siblings, spouses and children for the sake of Jesus[4] simply means that preference is due to what is the most important, namely the ultimate life which can be reached only in the footsteps of the Master. Once again, the emphasis is not on the target but on the action leading towards it.

A further rather particular mention of 'eternal life' may be found in the Gospel of Matthew; it figures at the end of the parable of the last judgement: 'And they will go away into eternal punishment, but the righteous into eternal life' (Mt 25:31–46). The scene recalls the Similitudes of Enoch, a book probably contemporaneous with and possibly influencing Matthew, where the Son of Man or the Elect condemns the sinners to destruction. Though not expressly stated, it presupposes the resurrection both of the righteous and of the wicked, followed by divine retribution to all.

It is to be borne in mind that with the possible exception of the last example, 'life' and 'eternal life' are never actually associated with resurrection or even necessarily imply the idea of it. So when, on rare occasions, Jesus spoke of eternal life, it is possible that he meant immortality. Also those Jews who thought they belonged to the final period (and Jesus was definitely one of them), believed that the

77

reign of God was on the point of bursting into this world. Consequently they imagined that they could pass into the 'age to come' without experiencing death and therefore needed no resurrection (Mk 9:1; Mt 16:28; Lk 9:27). Indeed we know that according to the teaching of Jesus, the kingdom of God was 'at hand' (Mk 1:15; Mt 4:17) and was already in the midst of his generation (Lk 17:20–21), as revealed by the charismatic exorcisms and healings performed by him and his envoys (Mt 11:4–5; Lk 7:22; Mt 10:7–8).

These few quotations from the first three Gospels obviously lead to the conclusion that the subject did not play a major role in Jesus' teaching as reflected in the Synoptics. It was only in the context of the eschatological end of time (which after the death of Jesus was developed by St Paul and the early Church to encourage belief in resurrection) that the topic acquired a climactic position in the thought of early Christianity. An examination of the part played by the concept of eternal life in the Fourth Gospel will help us to grasp its rising momentum.

ii. The Gospel of John

Compared to the four passages in the Synoptics, John's Gospel counts twenty-five occurrences of 'life' or 'eternal life' in the sayings ascribed to Jesus. The acts which in John are thus rewarded in most cases differ from those in the Synoptics. It is true there is one passage where 'life' is said to be earned by a hard-working harvester through his devotion to duty: 'He who reaps receives wages, and gathers fruit for **eternal life**' (Jn 4:36). And on another occasion 'eternal life' is the prize granted to a man who, inspired by outstanding moral heroism, sacrifices all his worldly values (Jn 11:25). However, most of the time, 'life', a kind of continued and renewed existence with God, is ultimately the reward of faith in Jesus, and/or in God the Father, who has sent Jesus: 'For God so loved the world that he gave his only Son, that whoever believes in him should not perish but have **eternal life**' (Jn 3:16). The same theme is repeated again and again in John: 'He who believes in the Son has **eternal life**; he who does not obey the Son shall not see **life**, but the wrath of God rests upon him' (Jn 3:36). Finally, presenting both Christ and God as the source of the gift, 'eternal life' is promised to those who hear the word of Jesus and believe in the Father who sent him (Jn 5:24).

In addition to the passages where belief in Jesus is the recipe for gaining eternal life, John includes a whole series of symbolical images where Jesus is depicted as the **fountain of life**. He is 'the spring of water welling up to eternal life' (Jn 4:14); 'the food which endures to eternal life' (Jn 6:27); 'the bread of life' (Jn 6:35, 48) his 'flesh' and 'blood' give 'eternal life' (Jn 6:53–54) and he is the 'light of life' (Jn 8:12). It will come in useful later on to remember that belief not only in Jesus, present among the faithful, but also in the name of Jesus, no longer in tangible contact with his disciples, was considered to give them life: 'These are written that you may believe that Jesus is the Christ, the Son of God, and that believing you may have **life in his name**' (Jn 20:31).

In John, as in the Synoptic Gospels, with the possible exception of Matthew's account of the last judgement (Mt 25:46), only the Jewish followers of Jesus are promised eternal life. We have to wait first until the charismatic conversion of the Roman centurion Cornelius and ultimately until the acceptance of the apostolic mission of

Paul in the Graeco-Roman world before encountering for the first time the possibility of non-Jews being judged worthy of eternal life without being compelled to pass through Judaism.

Whereas in the Synoptics Jesus is painted as the guiding light to the kingdom of God and in it to eternal life, in John we witness a more advanced stage of doctrinal development. Eternal life can be inherited by those who believe, not just in the words of Jesus the teacher, but in his heavenly power deriving from his special relationship with God the Father.

In conclusion, it must be recalled that Jesus' eschatological imagery in Mark, Matthew and Luke is centred not on resurrection,[5] but on the idea of the 'kingdom of God' or 'kingdom of heaven'. This is revealed by the frequency of the two formulae in the Synoptic Gospels where they appear more than eighty times as against two occurrences in a single passage of the Gospel of John (Jn 3:3, 5). Resurrection is an uncommon concept in the authentic message of Jesus revealed by the Synoptics, and the source of its central significance in Christian ideology must be sought elsewhere (see chapter 13). As for 'eternal life', while only sporadically used in the Synoptics, it gains increasing momentum and import in the Gospel of John.

8

Predictions of the resurrection of Jesus

All three Synoptic evangelists emphatically state that during the final period of his life Jesus repeatedly announced to his closest disciples his death and his resurrection. The Gospel of John contains nothing comparable. In it only an obscure forewarning is given, not to the apostles, but privately to Nicodemus, in the form of a symbolical reinterpretation of an Old Testament image, the brazen serpent which was set up by Moses in the wilderness as a talisman to protect against snake bites (Num 21:6–9). As it saved the Jews who looked at it with trust, so will the 'uplifted' (crucified, risen and glorified) Jesus give eternal life to the believers (Jn 3:14). We find another cryptic reference in Matthew's treatment of the sign of Jonah, alluding to the duration of Jesus' stay in the tomb before his resurrection: 'For as Jonah was three days and three nights in the belly of the whale, so will the Son of man be three days and three nights in the heart of the earth' (Mt 12:40).

Elsewhere Mark, Matthew and Luke are less mysterious. With greater or smaller detail they make Jesus foretell the events of the end of his life. The first occasion is Peter's confession at Caesarea Philippi of the Messiahship of Jesus acknowledged by all the apostles:

*And he began to teach them that the Son of man must suffer many things, and be rejected by the elders and the chief priests and the scribes, and be killed, and **after three days rise again*** (Mk 8:30–31).

Jesus forbade Peter to proclaim that he was the Christ and in the form of a tacit denial of the confession, he emphatically foretold the tragedy of his end and his rising from the dead.

In one or possibly two of the six occurrences, the last of them dated to two days before Passover, the forewarning is restricted to the arrest and the cross with no mention of the resurrection (Lk 9:44; Mt 26:2). Luke 9:22 repeats almost word for word the statement of Mark as quoted above (Mk 8:30–31) and so does Matthew too (Mt 16:21). Peter's reaction is at odds with the story which includes the resurrection. He 'rebukes' Jesus: 'God forbid, Lord! This shall never happen to you', a reproach that in turn provokes Jesus' angry riposte and disapproval of Peter: 'Get behind me, Satan!' (Mt 16:22–23; Mk 8:32–33).

The second, indirect prediction is associated with Jesus' order to the three leading apostles, Peter, James and John, who have accompanied him to the Galilean mountain of the Transfiguration, not to divulge their experience until he has risen from the dead (Mk 9:9; Mt 17:9). The extraordinary clarity of the announcement is offset by Mark's remark that the apostles had no idea what rising from the dead meant which, in turn, confirms our finding that resurrection had had no prominent part in Jesus' previous teaching.

The third premonition is also situated in Galilee. It is couched in generic terms – Jesus will be delivered into the hands of unspecified 'men' – and as in the previous case, the apostles did not know what he was talking about, but contrary to their habit, they were afraid to inquire (Mk 9:30–32; Mt 17:22–23; Lk 9:43–45).

The fourth episode is set during Jesus' last trip to Jerusalem, just a few days before Good Friday. In Mark's version it has all the appearances of a prophecy after the fact, mirroring in detail all the stages of the Passion, the arrest by the chief priests, the condemnation to death, the handing over to the Gentiles (the Romans), the mocking, spitting on and scourging, the execution and the rising from the dead on the third day.

In Luke, instead of adhering to the customary style of a direct prediction by Jesus, we encounter for the first time a reference to the fulfilment of prophecies: 'Behold, we are going up to Jerusalem, and everything that is written of the Son of man by the prophets will be accomplished' (Lk 18:31). The same formula is repeated later in Luke, first in the conversation of the risen Jesus with the disciples on the way to Emmaus:

O foolish men, and slow to believe all that the prophets have spoken! Was it not necessary that the Christ should suffer these things and enter into his glory? (Lk 24:25).

And later in Jesus' address to the apostles in Jerusalem:

These are my words which I spoke to you, while I was still with you, that everything written about me in the law of Moses and the prophets and the psalms must be fulfilled (Lk 24:44).

In the last, straightforward prediction, a couple of days before the crucifixion, Jesus foretells in Jerusalem his impending arrest and death: 'You know that after two days the Passover is coming, and the Son of man will be delivered up to be crucified' (Mt 26:2).

If we leave aside the examples of the brazen serpent and the sign of Jonah, all the predictions are couched in clear and simple language that no one could possibly misunderstand. It is hardly possible that they did not hear the message. Indeed, on one occasion Jesus is said to have explicitly drawn the apostles' attention to what he was going to tell them: 'Let these words sink into your ears; for the Son of man is to be delivered into the hands of men' (Lk 9:44).

In the circumstances, it is remarkable that the evangelists time and again assert, as we have shown above, that the disciples found the announcements of Jesus incomprehensible:

They kept the matter to themselves, questioning what the rising from the dead meant (Mk 9:10).

They did not understand the saying, and they were afraid to ask him (Mk 9:32; Lk 9:44).

But they understood none of these things; this saying was hid from them, and they did not grasp what was said (Lk 18:34).

Later we learn something even more bizarre. The women friends of Jesus had actually forgotten what appears to have been their Master's most momentous statement until two angels in human appearance refreshed their memory (Lk 24:8).

One detail of the prediction is reiterated several times: the resurrection was expected to take place either 'on the third day' or 'after three days'. The typology of Jonah involves three days and three nights, corresponding to the time spent by the fugitive prophet in the belly of the big fish (Mt 12:40). Mark, on the other hand, speaks of 'after three days' (8:31; 9:31; 10:34) and Matthew and Luke refer to 'the third day' (Mt 16:21; 17:22; 20:19; Lk 9:22; 18:33; 24:46).

According to our way of counting, three days mean three 24-hour periods, but Jesus did not remain that long in his grave, as he was buried late afternoon on Friday and the resurrection is placed by the evangelists before dawn on Sunday. The phrase of Matthew and Luke, 'on the third day', would suit this reckoning, but it is more likely that the expression was chosen because it was a typical Old Testament formula marking seven significant biblical events occurring 'on the third day'. Among these are Abraham's discovery of the site of the sacrifice of Isaac: 'On the third day Abraham lifted up his eyes and saw the place afar off' (Gen 22:4) and Hosea's prophecy of the resurrection, 'After two days, he will revive us, on the third day he will raise us up' (Hos 6:2). One should also take into account that according to rabbinic reckoning part of a day or night counted as a full day or night (yShabbath 2a; bPesahim 4a).

There may have been another reason in favour of the choice of the third day. According to an ancient Jewish belief, after death the departed soul did not wish to abandon the body and was keen to rejoin it. Hence for three days it continued to hover over the body or kept on revisiting the grave (Genesis Rabba 100:7; yYebamoth 15c).

The predictions of the resurrection of Jesus and the reactions ascribed to the disciples are filled with oddities. Contrary to what we have found in connection with the surviving sayings of Jesus about afterlife, they suddenly turn resurrection into an issue of central importance, one that was forecast not only by Jesus, but also foreseen and foretold by the prophets of the Old Testament. In other words, the execution and subsequent resurrection of Jesus were part of his foreknowledge and on account of the relevant 'prophecies', belonged to traditional Jewish messianic expectation. If so, the arrest, crucifixion and resurrection of Jesus could not have come out of the blue. On the contrary, they must have been dead certainties for his apostles and disciples.

Yet all the four Gospels prove the contrary. The cross and the resurrection were unexpected, perplexing, indeed incomprehensible for the apostles. When Jesus was captured in the garden of Gethsemane, his apostles abandoned him and fled, at least according to the testimony of the Synoptic evangelists.[1] Peter even denied that he had known Jesus. As for the resurrection, no one was awaiting it, nor were the apostles willing to believe the good news brought to them by the women who had visited the tomb of Jesus.

In fact, we have two sets of evidence which contradict one another with no possibility for reconciliation, since it is hardly likely that the dishonourable behaviour of the apostles does not correspond to reality and is a mere invention. One must conclude that the predictions by Jesus of his death and resurrection and his reference to biblical prophecies about his suffering and glorification are inauthentic. They appear to represent the tracing back to Jesus of some of the weapons of the apologetical-polemical arsenal of the Jewish-Christian Church: Jesus informed his confidants about the cross and the resurrection, which could also be guessed by enlightened readers of the Bible. The realization of the predictions proved to the apostles and to the members of the nascent Church that however astonishing the two events appeared, they were willed, foreordained and engineered by God.

9

Resurrection accounts in the New Testament regarding persons other than Jesus

The resurrection of Jesus is by no means the one and only revival story in the New Testament. In addition to rumours of a risen John the Baptist, the Gospels and the Acts of the Apostles mention five particular resuscitations: three are attributed to Jesus and one each to St Peter and St Paul.

When Jesus inquired from his apostles about who people thought he was, they referred to rumours according to which he was the reborn Elijah, Jeremiah or another biblical prophet. He was also held to be John the Baptist (Mk 8:28; Mt 16:14; Lk 9:19). A similar story circulated in Galilee in the court of Herod Antipas, purporting that Jesus was the reincarnation of John the Baptist, whom Antipas had executed (Mk 6:14–16; Mt 14:1–2; Lk 9:7–9). The expectation of the return of Elijah was part of Old Testament tradition: the prophet Malachi spoke of God dispatching again his messenger, Elijah (Mal 3:1; 4:5), and the New Testament also associates John the Baptist with the risen Elijah (Mk 1:2).

The first of the resuscitations reported in the Synoptics, that of the daughter of a certain Jairus, is placed at the beginning of the Galilean career of Jesus. There is uncertainty among the evangelists about the identity of the father, who approached Jesus (Mk 5:21–43; Mt 9:18–26; Lk 40–56). While all agree that he was called Jairus, or Yair in Hebrew, Mark and Luke describe him as the president of a local synagogue, whereas in Matthew he is a nameless 'ruler', an important figure, no doubt belonging to the local council of elders. In Matthew the girl is already dead and the father invites Jesus to come to his house and raise her. In the other two Gospels she is on the point of dying and the news of her death reaches the father during his conversation with Jesus. Although Jesus tries to disguise the miraculous quality of his intervention and equivocally refers to her condition as sleep, a designation that serves also as a metaphor for death, the sarcastic reaction of the attendants makes clear that by the time of the arrival of the miracle-worker, the twelve-year-old young woman was no longer among the living (Lk 8:53).

According to Mark and Luke, the performance of Jesus' miracle is witnessed by three apostles and the parents of the girl. Like healings and exorcisms, the resuscitation too was brought about by a command, *Talitha cum*,[1] reproduced in Aramaic in Mark and followed by a slightly expanded Greek translation, 'Little girl, I say to you, arise!' In Luke it appears only in straight literal Greek, 'Child, arise!' In Matthew, the revivification was preceded by bodily contact. Meeting Jesus, the father asked him to lay his hands on the dead girl and on their arrival in the house Jesus grasped her hand and raised her up. Luke expressly states that the spirit returned to her, implying thereby that she rose from the dead rather than just woke up from a coma. In conformity with his habit, Jesus forbade the divulgation of the miracle, but predictably the rumour of it spread in the neighbouring districts.

The second raising of the dead, transmitted only by Luke, is said to have happened in full publicity in Nain, an otherwise unknown Galilean village situated not far from

Capernaum. It was observed by Jesus' disciples and a great crowd. At the gate of the locality, Jesus and his followers met a funeral cortège carrying a young man, the only son of a widowed mother. Once more, the raising of the dead is performed by touch and speech. Jesus put his hand on the bier and issued the order, 'Young man, I say to you, arise!', probably 'Talya qum' in Aramaic. When the dead youth sat up and started to speak, the onlookers proclaimed Jesus a great prophet and, as one would expect, the news was broadcast far and wide in the country (Lk 7:11–17).

These resuscitations recall the Old Testament stories of Elijah and Elisha (see pp. 30–32). While the reviving of the son of the widow from Zarephath and the son of the Shunamite woman increased the fame of the ancient prophets as miracle-workers, nothing is said about the further life of the two young men. Likewise, in the Galilee of the first century AD, the reputation of Jesus continued to grow after his raising of a girl and a young man, but neither the daughter of Jairus nor the resuscitated youth from Nain is mentioned thereafter. Similarly, no recipient of Jesus' charismatic healing and exorcistic activity is referred to again, with the exception of Mary Magdalene, out of whom Jesus is said to have expelled seven demons (Lk 8:2; Mk 16:9).

In the Synoptic Gospels, as well as in the Acts of the Apostles, raising the dead differs from the stories of Elijah and Elisha in so far as it is connected with the final period preceding the establishment of the kingdom of God. Thus in a message sent to the imprisoned John the Baptist, Jesus implied that his ministry was accompanied by the rising of the dead and foreshadowed the onset of the messianic age: 'The blind receive their sight and the lame walk, lepers are cleansed and **the dead are raised up** (Mt 11:4–5; Lk 7:22).

However, by the time of the Fourth Gospel, the outlook had changed and a clear distinction was made between 'the resurrection at the last day' (Jn 11:24) and the resuscitation of a person in what counted as the present time, as can be seen in the account of Lazarus. According to the story told by John (Jn 11:1–46), Lazarus had fallen ill, died and had already been buried for four days before Jesus arrived in Bethany, the home town of Lazarus and his sisters. By then the decomposition of the corpse had already started. Yet when Jesus cried out with a loud voice, 'Lazarus, come out!', the dead man, with his hands and feet bound, and his face wrapped with a cloth, rose and emerged from the tomb. The attendants had to unbind him before he could properly walk.

The principal discrepancy between John's report and the Synoptics relates to the aftermath of this resurrection. In the Synoptics the resurrected persons are assumed to live on, yet they disappear over the horizon. They are simply the beneficiaries of the miracle-working activity of the holy man. By contrast, we learn from the fourth evangelist that many Jews, friends and neighbours who came to comfort the bereaved sisters of Lazarus, saw what happened and made the story public, thus turning not only Jesus, but even Lazarus, into a celebrity. So when the raised Lazarus was sitting at the table at a dinner party in the company of Jesus, a great local crowd surrounded the house, eager to see the former dead man enjoying a meal next to the prophet who had restored him to life. According to John, the impact of the sight had led many Jews to believe in Jesus, and this nearly brought a premature second death to Lazarus. We are told that the chief priests, in order to stop the growing popularity of Jesus, were plotting the assassination of Lazarus (Jn 12:9–11).[2]

As has been noted, according to the Synoptic Gospels, charismatic power was not the exclusive privilege of Jesus. He is reported as sharing it with his disciples right from the beginning of his Galilean activity. When the twelve apostles were sent on their first missionary tour, they were commanded to preach, heal the sick, cleanse lepers, expel evil spirits and **raise the dead** (Mt 10:7–8). In fact, a case of resuscitation is attributed on a later occasion to Peter, who restored to life a charitable woman disciple from Joppa, called 'Deer' – Tabitha in Aramaic and Dorcas in Greek (Acts 9:36–41). Paul matched Peter's performance and apparently revived Eutychus, a young man from the Mysenian coastal city of Troas in Asia Minor. The unfortunate youth fell to his death from a third-storey window after dozing off during Paul's overlong after-dinner speech (Acts 20:7–10). We do not hear of either of them again, but their stories serve to illustrate the continuing charisma in the early Jesus movement which enveloped the ministry of Jesus and of his apostles and disciples with a splendid messianic aura.

How were such resurrection stories received by first-century AD Palestinian Jews? Josephus may help to answer this question. His depiction of the extraordinary miracles of the prophet Elisha, which many of Josephus' co-religionists have accepted as established facts, gives a valuable insight into the mentality of the age. No doubt the sophisticated Josephus preferred to sit on the fence, especially as he was addressing a Roman readership:

Now I have written about these matters as I have found them in my readings; if anyone wishes to judge otherwise of them, I shall not object to his holding a different opinion (Ant 10:281).

However, popular Jewish circles in the age of Jesus were without such scruples. They happily accepted miracles and some of them joined the Jesus movement and believed in the resurrection of Christ despite the problematic character of the Gospel evidence as we shall outline in the next chapter.

Appendix

A token resurrection after the death of Jesus

A unique and otherwise unclassifiable incident is reported by Matthew as coinciding with the death of Jesus on the cross. According to his Gospel, the tragic event was marked by an earthquake, a common feature together with thunder, tornado and fire, of the eschatological crescendo in scripture (Isa 29:6; Ps 18:7; Mk 13:8; Mt 24:7; Lk 21:11). Following this earthquake, rocks were split and tombs were opened. Out of them emerged the risen bodies of many saints who were seen by numerous inhabitants of Jerusalem following the resurrection of Jesus (Mt 27:51–53). Needless to say, nothing is heard of them afterwards.

Matthew's account is best understood as symbolical and suggests that an anticipatory resurrection, the disgorging of the raised 'saints' (i.e. righteous) by the gaping tombs, happened immediately after Jesus had expired. Yet the saints are said to have appeared to 'many', not on Friday, but early on Sunday. Therefore the religious message hints at a link between the death and consequent resurrection of Jesus and the general raising of the dead. This idea points to St Paul's definition of the rising of Jesus as the 'first fruits' of the general resurrection. It is to be observed that Matthew speaks again of an earthquake at the moment of the resurrection of Jesus (Mt 28:2). There is no further reference to the story in New Testament tradition.

10

The Gospel accounts of the resurrection of Jesus

Preliminary: The burial of Jesus[1]

The three Synoptics, Mark, Matthew and Luke, report that at the approach of nightfall on Friday, 15 Nisan, Joseph of Arimathea, a member of the Sanhedrin and a crypto-sympathizer of Jesus, obtained permission from the Roman governor to take down the body from the cross. The centurion in command of the execution squad testified before Pontius Pilate that Jesus had already died, and Joseph was granted permission to proceed with a hasty burial. Without the use of the customary spices, he wrapped the body in a linen shroud. He then laid it in a freshly hewn rock tomb, the entrance of which was protected by a large and heavy rollable stone. Mary Magdalene and another woman, also named Mary, and one more or several further Galilean women are said to have watched Joseph of Arimathea burying Jesus (Mk 15:42–47; Mt 27:57–61; Lk 23:50–56).

The tradition transmitted by John partly disagrees with the Synoptics. The crucifixion takes place on 14, not 15, Nisan. Joseph of Arimathea is helped by a second secret disciple of Jesus, Nicodemus, to lay Jesus in the tomb (Jn 3:2). Nicodemus brings a linen shroud, together with a large quantity of spices, and the two hurriedly place Jesus in a new tomb in the midst of a garden, without being observed by any woman witness (Jn 19:38–42). In John's account there is no need for the women's services as Jesus' body has already been anointed by the two men.

Matthew, unlike the other evangelists, further notes that the Jewish leaders, fearing that the disciples of Jesus might steal his body to fake the fulfilment of his predicted resurrection, ask Pilate to keep the tomb under military guard. The governor leaves the matter in their hands and the chief priests post sentries at the tomb after sealing the entrance of the grave.

Thus the scene is set for the story of the resurrection. The evidence will be considered in reverse chronological order, starting with John, the latest of the Gospels, and finishing with Mark, the earliest.

1. The resurrection in John

Chapters 20 and 21 of the Fourth Gospel recount the resurrection of Jesus and the appearances that followed it. With chapter 20 ends John's original account, stating:

Now Jesus did many other signs in the presence of the disciples, which are not written in this book; but these are written that you may believe that Jesus is the Christ, the Son of God, and that believing you may have life in his name (Jn 20:30–31).

Chapter 21 has its own particular conclusion, which reveals its supplementary nature:

But there are also many other things which Jesus did; were every one of them to be written, I suppose that the world itself could not contain the books that would be written (Jn 21:25).

John offers the most detailed picture of the purported apparitions of the risen Jesus. His narrative consists of eight stages:

1. Early on Sunday morning, 'while it was still dark', Mary Magdalene, without being accompanied by other Galilean women, went to the burial place and found it open, with the stone rolled away (Jn 20:1).

2. At once she reported to Peter and the anonymous 'beloved disciple' that the body of Jesus had been moved by unknown people. 'They have taken the Lord out of the tomb, and we do not know where they have laid him' (Jn 20:2).

3. The two men ran to the sepulchre and Peter, who entered first, noticed only the linen cloths and the napkin separately folded, but saw no body. The 'beloved disciple' is said to have at once 'believed', although at that moment neither he nor Peter knew that Christ's resurrection had been predicted either by Jesus or by the scriptures. Thereupon, according to John, both left the place and went home without saying a word or expressing any surprise or emotion (Jn 20:3–10).

4. By contrast, Mary Magdalene, who had followed Peter and his companion to the garden, remained there weeping. Peering into the tomb, she saw two angels, and when they asked her why she was crying, she told them that someone had removed the body of Jesus and transferred it to an unknown location. The angels made no comment (Jn 20:11–13).

5. Next, Mary became aware of the presence of a man standing behind her, whom she took for the gardener in charge of the burial ground. Presuming that it was he who had displaced the body, she inquired where he had put it, so that she could take it away. When the presumed gardener addressed her as 'Mary', she identified him as Jesus and called him in Aramaic 'Rabbuni', my Master. She was ordered by the visually unrecognizable Jesus not to cling to him as he had not yet gone to the Father and he told her to inform the apostles about his impending ascent on high (Jn 20:20:17). So Mary Magdalene hastened to the disciples and reported to them all that she had seen and heard (Jn 20:14–18).

6. Mary Magdalene's vision was followed by the appearance of Jesus to the disciples on the same evening. Although the doors were shut, he entered the house and breathed on them the Holy Spirit, thus granting them power to pardon or retain sins in the course of their apostolic mission (Jn 20:19–23).

7. Thomas the Twin, who was not present, did not trust his colleagues' testimony:

But he said to them, 'Unless I see in his hands the print of the nails, and place my finger in the mark of the nails, and place my hand in his side, I will not believe' (Jn 20:19–25).

8. Eight days later, the figure of Jesus was seen re-entering the house despite the shut doors, and he invited Thomas to touch his wounds. He did so and believed (Jn 20:26–29).

John's account of the resurrection is followed by an additional episode, in which a third apparition to some disciples takes place not in Jerusalem, but in Galilee, by the Sea of Tiberias. Seven apostles spent the whole night fishing without catching anything. At dawn they saw a man on the beach, but like Mary Magdalene, they did not recognize him as Jesus until the 'beloved disciple' told them that he was the Lord (Jn 21:1–7).

The rest of the chapter is not directly relevant to the resurrection story. It goes without saying that John is substantially at variance with the Synoptics.

2. The resurrection in Luke

Luke's resurrection narrative, nearly as long as John's, is made up of five parts:

1. Mary Magdalene, Joanna and Mary the mother of James, together with other Galilean women disciples, arrived at the tomb early on Sunday to anoint the body. They knew the place, having kept Joseph of Arimathea under observation two days earlier. They found the stone rolled away and the tomb empty. Two men in glittering clothes suddenly appeared and reminded them of Jesus' earlier predictions:

Remember how he told you, while he was still in Galilee, that the Son of man must be delivered into the hands of sinful men, and be crucified, and on the third day rise (Lk 24:6).

Mary Magdalene and her friends informed the eleven apostles, but they haughtily shrugged off their words as women's silly tales (Lk 24:1–12).

2. On the same Sunday, Cleopas and another disciple travelled from Jerusalem to the village of Emmaus and were discussing the tragedy of Jesus. They met a stranger on the road, who did not seem to know anything about the events that had shaken up Jerusalem during the previous days. The disciples put him in the picture, told him of the empty tomb and about the women hearing from angels that Jesus was alive, and that some of their male colleagues had confirmed the disappearance of the body. At that juncture, the stranger proceeded to demonstrate to them from the scriptures that the Messiah had first to suffer and then be glorified. They invited him to stay with them in Emmaus and during the meal they were sharing, at the sight of some unspecified idiosyncrasy in the stranger's benediction ritual, it dawned on them that their travelling companion was Jesus. But by then he had vanished.

The two disciples at once rejoined the apostles and their associates in Jerusalem, but even before they could report what they had seen, they were told that Jesus had appeared to Peter (Lk 24:13–35).

3. At that moment the apostles and disciples saw a ghost: 'They were startled and frightened, and supposed that they saw a spirit' (Lk 24:37).

This ghost turned out to be Jesus, whose wounded hands and feet could be touched. To prove his real humanity, he asked for food and ate some fish before their eyes (Lk 24:36–43).

4. The risen Jesus then explained to them all the scriptural predictions that related to him in the Law, the Prophets and the Psalms, and ordered the apostles to evangelize in his name across the whole world (Lk 24:46). To make the story consistent with the Acts of the Apostles, where the Ascension takes place forty days after Easter,

the apostles are also commanded not to leave Jerusalem until they have received the Holy Spirit (Lk 24:49).

5. Yet apparently on the same day, the Sunday of the resurrection, Jesus took them out of Jerusalem to Bethany, where they saw him rising to heaven (Lk 24:50–53).

3. The resurrection in Matthew

The account of Matthew, consisting of seven sections, is considerably shorter than those of John and Luke:

1. Two women, Mary Magdalene and 'the other Mary' (no doubt the mother of James, as in Luke 24:10), went to the tomb on Sunday towards dawn. As they are not said to be carrying spices, we must surmise that their visit was motivated by piety (Mt 28:1).

2. In the course of an earthquake, an angel, wearing shiny white garments, rolled back the stone from the opening of the rock cavity and sat on it. The guards posted there by the chief priests 'trembled and became like dead men' (Mt 28:2–4).

3. The angel reassured the frightened women and announced that Jesus had risen, hence the empty tomb, and ordered them to report the news to the disciples and instruct them to meet Jesus in Galilee (Mt 28:5–7).

4. Frightened as well as delighted, the women immediately set out to do as they were told, and on the way they had a vision of Jesus, who repeated to them the angel's instructions (Mt 28:8–10).

5. When the guards recovered their senses, they went to tell the chief priests about the disappearance of the body of Jesus. The priests bribed them to pretend that

the apostles had stolen the corpse during the night. This rumour continued to circulate among the Jews even in Matthew's day (Mt 28:11–15).

6. Jesus was not seen in Jerusalem. The only vision the eleven apostles experienced was on a Galilean mountain. On that occasion, some of them believed, but others did not (Mt 28:16–17).

7. The resurrection narrative and the Gospel end with the risen Jesus commissioning his disciples to baptize all the nations (Mt 28:18–20).

4. The resurrection in Mark

The oldest codices of Mark's Gospel, the Sinaiticus and the Vaticanus (fourth century AD), as well as the old Sinaitic Syriac translation (fourth/fifth century), abruptly terminate chapter 16 at verse 8. This is the so-called shorter ending of Mark. The longer ending (Mk 16:9–19), a later revision of the account, will follow in section b.

(a) The shorter ending
This compact finale of Mark constitutes by far the briefest account of Jesus' rising from the dead. In fact, the generally agreed chronological sequence of the four Gospels, Mark, Matthew, Luke, John, presents a progressively developing description of the resurrection. Three stages can be distinguished in the chain of events as recorded in Mark 16:1–8.

1. Three women, Mary Magdalene, Mary the mother of James and Salome,[2] went to the tomb of Jesus before sunrise on Sunday with spices to anoint his body, wondering

how they would be able to remove the heavy stone from the entrance (Mk 16:1–3).

2. They found the stone rolled back and saw inside the tomb a young man seated and robed in a white garment, from whom they learned that Jesus was no longer in his grave. The women were commanded to announce his resurrection to the apostles and tell them to meet him in Galilee (Mk 16:4–7).

3. Terrified, they did not follow the order and kept the story to themselves:

They went out and fled from the tomb; for trembling and astonishment had come upon them; and they said nothing to any one, for they were afraid (Mk 16:8).

The Gospel dramatically breaks off on this note of suspense. Mark abstains altogether from mentioning any resurrection appearance. However, a later editor or editors of the chapter who appended the longer ending felt it necessary to smooth down the ruggedness of Mark's story and fill in the gaps under the influence of the Gospels of Luke and John.

(b) The longer ending

The longer ending completes the main gap and inserts into Mark's narrative several apparitions of the risen Jesus:

1. Early on Sunday, Jesus revealed himself in a vision to Mary Magdalene, out of whom he had previously expelled seven demons (see Lk 8:2). Mary reported the matter to the grieving apostles, but they refused to believe her (Mk 16:9–11).

2. The longer ending makes Jesus appear in the country

to two travelling disciples, as he did in Luke's Emmaus episode. Without delay, they acquainted the apostles with their experience, but their report, like that of Mary Magdalene, fell on deaf ears (Mk 16:12–13).

3. Next, Jesus appeared in a vision to the eleven apostles and rebuked them for their lack of faith in the testimony of Mary Magdalene and the two travellers (Mk 16:14).

4. The vision ends with the risen Jesus ordering the apostles to proclaim the message of the Gospel to the whole world and promising to them the gift of charismatic powers to be exercised in his name (Mk 16:15–18).

5. Then, seemingly on the same day, Jesus was lifted up to heaven to sit at God's right hand (see also Lk 24:51). The disciples, in turn, departed to preach the Gospel and confirmed their message by the charismatic miracles guaranteed to them by Jesus (Mk 16:19–20).

Appendix

The Ascension

Since the longer ending of Mark's resurrection story and that of Luke contain a description of Jesus' ascent to heaven, it is appropriate to include here some comments on the account of the Ascension given by Luke in the opening chapter of the Acts of the Apostles. The three sources yield conflicting data.

1. In the dedication of the Acts of the Apostles to his patron, Theophilus (see also Lk 1:3), Luke refers to his 'first book' – the Gospel – dealing with Jesus' life and teaching up to the moment of his elevation to heaven, seemingly on Easter Sunday. According to this second

book, Jesus stayed with his disciples for forty days after his resurrection, instructing them about the kingdom of God, during which period they remained in Jerusalem and waited for the Holy Spirit (Acts 1:1–5).[3]

2. While refusing to reveal to the apostles the moment of the restoration of the kingdom of Israel, no doubt identical with the inauguration of God's kingdom, Jesus promised them the charismatic gift of the Holy Spirit in order to make them his witnesses among Jews and Gentiles (Acts 1:6–8).

3. From the Mount of Olives (Acts 1:12), he was then borne heavenwards by a cloud until he disappeared from the sight of the apostles. At once two white-robed men (angelic beings?) materialized and announced that he would return: 'This Jesus, who was taken up from you into heaven, will come in the same way as you saw him go into heaven' (Acts 1:11).

The sketches assembled in this chapter constitute the sum total of the New Testament's 'documentary' evidence concerning the resurrection of Jesus.

All that remains now is to assess the reports included in the Gospels and supplement them with the relevant extracts from the Acts, Paul and the rest of the New Testament material.[4] The existing interpretations represent the full scale of the spectrum. To quote the two extremes, N. T. Wright, the learned twenty-first-century Bishop of Durham, author of a disquisition of over 800 pages, concludes that the resurrection of Jesus was a historical event.[5] By contrast, the more succinct David Friedrich Strauss, one of the creators of the historico-critical approach to the Gospels in the nineteenth century, declares that 'rarely has an incredible fact been worse attested, and never has a badly attested fact been intrinsically less credible'.[6]

11

Initial evaluation of the accounts of the resurrection of Jesus

While a full appraisal of the New Testament evidence concerning the meaning of Jesus' resurrection will have to wait until chapter 15 and the Epilogue, our preliminary task here is to clarify the confused and often contradictory data contained in the Gospels and in chapter 1 of the Acts of the Apostles.

The uncertainties concern the sequence of the events, the identity of the informants and witnesses, the number and location of the apparitions of Jesus, the presentation of prophecies relating to the resurrection and finally the date of Jesus' purported departure from earth. The discrepancies among the various accounts regarding both details and substance cannot have escaped the eyes of attentive readers.

The most significant peculiarity of the resurrection stories is that they nowhere suggest that the rising of Jesus from the dead was expected by anyone. In Matthew, Mark and John the resurrection complex is presented as falling straight out of the blue, a complete surprise. Luke mentions Jesus' earlier announcement of his rising that was either misunderstood or forgotten (!?!) by his disciples.

The most irreconcilable versions are yielded by John on the one hand, and by Mark's shorter ending – or Mark A – on the other.

In John's narrative the removal of the stone from the grave is not linked to the idea of resurrection, but is attributed by Mary Magdalene to some unknown person who had entered it and had taken away the body of Jesus. The idea of resurrection does not arise at all in her report to two apostles. Neither is there any hint at resurrection in the conversation between Mary Magdalene and the two angels.

At the other extreme, Mark A offers as the sole source of the story of the resurrection the words of an unknown young man clad in white (an angel?). The women are told that the tomb is empty because Jesus has risen. Mary Magdalene and her two friends communicate their experience to no one. There is no reference to any vision of Jesus in Mark A, just as there is no allusion to the empty tomb in Paul's account in 1 Corinthians 15.

Characteristically, Jesus was never identified in any of his appearances. Mary Magdalene took him for the gardener and the disciples travelling to Emmaus, and the apostles by the Sea of Tiberias, thought he was a stranger. In Jerusalem the apostles believed they were seeing a ghost. The risen Christ did not display the familiar features of Jesus of Nazareth.

Going through the stories, stage by stage, each of them contains unique elements missing from the other Gospels. Some of them lack parallels, others attest details that are irreconcilable:

1. In John, Mary Magdalene ventures alone to the tomb and conveys her discovery of the disappearance of Jesus' body to Peter and the 'beloved disciple'. Peter and his companion do not trust Mary and go to check her report. The 'beloved disciple' *believes*, but we are not told exactly

what he believes. By implication, this means that Peter does not share his belief. Still in John, Mary Magdalene announces to the apostles that Jesus is going to the Father, apparently excluding the possibility of a further stay with them, let alone of a visit to Galilee. However, this statement is contradicted in John's additional account in chapter 21, where Jesus meets some of his apostles by the Sea of Tiberias. In Matthew, a Galilean mountain is the only place where Jesus appears to the apostles. In Mark A a visit to Galilee is announced by the young man in the tomb, but the matter is dropped there and then. Unparalleled are the confirmation of Peter's leading position among the apostles, and the two episodes relating to Thomas as recorded in John.

2. Luke's particular contribution consists in his emphasis on the prophecies announcing the resurrection. The two men (angels?) seen by the women at the tomb recall Jesus' prediction of his suffering and rising and in both his conversation with the disciples on the road to Emmaus and during his appearance to the apostles in Jerusalem Jesus expounds the biblical prophecies foretelling his resurrection. Peter's prominence is indicated by a special vision of Jesus, exclusive to him, prior to the return of the disciples from Emmaus and the apostles' vision of Christ in Jerusalem. Is this the apparition to Peter mentioned later by Paul (1 Cor 15:5)?

3. In his resurrection account Matthew speaks of the guards fainting when the angel opens the tomb in the midst of an earthquake and of their later report of the event to the chief priests. Also peculiar to Matthew is the claim, attributed to the priests, that the apostles have stolen the corpse, and the reference to the continued circulation of the rumour among hostile Jews at the time of Matthew's

writing his Gospel. A further detail attested only by Matthew concerns the appearance of Jesus to the two women who were bringing to the apostles the news of Jesus' resurrection. This is the only apparition of Jesus mentioned by Matthew as occurring in Jerusalem. Finally, only Matthew describes the meeting of Jesus with his apostles on a mountain in Galilee, and notes that several of them continued to harbour doubts, a detail left unresolved unlike John's story of Thomas, first doubting but later believing.

4. The unparalleled characteristics in the shorter ending of Mark are the evangelist's assertion that the frightened female witnesses of the empty tomb kept the story to themselves, and the complete absence of apparitions. In the longer ending of Mark, the unmatched remarks relate to the unwillingness of the apostles to believe the testimony of either Mary Magdalene or the disciples returning from Emmaus about their vision of Jesus, and to the detailed list of charismatic phenomena promised to the believers in the risen Christ.

Finally, there are flat contradictions between the sources:

1. The accounts differ regarding the number and identity of the women who visited the tomb: one, Mary Magdalene, in John and Mark B; two, Mary Magdalene and the other Mary, in Matthew; three, Mary Magdalene, Mary the mother of James and Salome, in Mark A; and several, Mary Magdalene, Joanna, Mary the mother of James and other women from Galilee, in Luke. Such variations would have rendered the testimony unacceptable in a Jewish law court.

2. The number of persons seen by the women at or in the tomb and the message they have received from them vary too. In John two angels appear to Mary Magdalene,

but they do not ask her to do anything. In Luke the two men remind the women of Christ's prophecy about his resurrection. In Matthew and in Mark A, the one angel entrusts Mary Magdalene and her friends with the duty to convey to the apostles the news of the resurrection of Jesus and an invitation to meet him in Galilee. However, in Mark the women do not obey this command; nor do we find there, not even in the longer ending, a reference to a trip to Galilee.

3. The number and the location of the apparitions of Jesus also greatly differ in the various Gospels. In Mark A there is none. In John, prior to his apparition to the apostles, Jesus shows himself to Mary Magdalene; in Matthew, to the women on their way to the apostles; in Luke to the two disciples in Emmaus and to Peter alone in Jerusalem, while Mark's longer ending speaks of apparitions of Jesus both to Mary Magdalene in Jerusalem and to the travelling disciples away from the capital. A vision by all the apostles occurring in Jerusalem is reported by Luke and Mark B (the longer version of Mark). The same is referred to in John, except that on the first occasion Thomas is absent and eight days later he is present. By contrast, according to Matthew, a Galilean mountain is the setting of the only apparition of Jesus to the apostles, while in John's supplementary evidence the Sea of Tiberias is the site of a final vision of Jesus by seven apostles. Luke, by contrast, expressly excludes any departure from Jerusalem, so for him no visionary encounter with Jesus can be situated in Galilee.

4. The apostolic mission is conferred on the disciples by the risen Jesus in Jerusalem according to John, Luke and the longer ending of Mark. According to Matthew this happens in Galilee. No actual meeting is stated in Mark A,

although a confusing mention of a promised encounter in Galilee figures in the instruction given by Mark's young man to the three women at the tomb.

5. Jesus' ascension to heaven takes place in Jerusalem in Mark B and by implication in John; in Bethany according to Luke; and on the Mount of Olives (in the area of Bethany) in the Acts of the Apostles. The sources are, however, at variance as regards the date of the event. Mark B puts it as Easter Sunday, but in the Acts it happens forty days later. Luke is equivocal. 'He led them out as far as Bethany' could be understood as immediately following Jesus' address to the apostles on the day of the resurrection, but the previous mention of staying in Jerusalem until they are 'clothed with power from on high' (an allusion to Pentecost) might suggest that Luke both in his Gospel and in the Acts allows nearly six weeks to elapse between Easter and the Ascension. In John, Jesus' journey to the Father is implied as happening on Easter Sunday, too.

In sum, a double argument is offered by the evangelists to prove the resurrection of Jesus. The first is the Synoptic version, based on the discovery of the empty tomb, and interpreted by one or two mysterious messengers as the proof that Jesus has risen. The legal value of this attestation is weakened by the fact that the witnesses are women. Female testimony, flippantly called nonsense (*lêros*) by the apostles in Luke, did not count in Jewish male society. Besides, the number and identity of the women witnesses remain in doubt. John and Luke try to improve the evidence by introducing two, or several, male witnesses (Peter and the 'beloved disciple' in John; 'some of those who were with us' in Luke) to confirm the women's report in so far as the disappearance of the body of Jesus is concerned. But, as will be shown in chapter 15, resurrection is not the only possible explanation of an empty tomb.

The second line of argument relies on visions and apparitions, which amount for those who accept them as first-hand evidence. But quite apart from the wide variations in the accounts regarding the time and place of the appearances and the identity of the visionaries, there are no *independent* witnesses from outside the circle of the followers of Jesus to corroborate them.[1] In fact, here and there we find hints indicating that even some of the insiders remained unconvinced. The risen Lazarus is said to have been seen moving, eating and drinking by all and sundry, friend and foe, so that the chief priests were thinking of eliminating him. Nothing similar is voiced about Jesus.

This glance at the evidence relative to the resurrection of Jesus ends on a perplexing note. We will return to it and to the theories it has generated after the investigation of the remainder of the material in the Acts of the Apostles, the letters of Saint Paul and the rest of the New Testament has been completed.

Synopsis of Parallels

MM = Mary Magdalene
BD = Beloved Disciple

ACTS	JOHN	LUKE	MATTHEW	MARK A	MARK B
	MM at tomb.	MM, Joanna & M mother of James.	MM + other Mary.	MM, Mary mother of James, Salome.	
	No spices.	Spices.	No spices.	Spices.	
			[Earthquake.]		
	Stone taken away.	Stone moved. 2 men seen. Reminded women of prophecies.	Stone moved by 1 angel. Tells women J gone. Apostles to meet him in Galilee.	Stone moved. 1 young man. J gone. Apostles to meet him in Galilee.	
			[Guards faint.]		
	[MM reports to Peter & Beloved Disciple that J's body removed.]				
		Women report to apostles. Disbelief.	Women frightened and joyful – run to apostles and report.	[Terrified women fled, not saying anything to anyone.]	
			[Vision of J on the way.]		[MM vision of J. Reports to apostles. Disbelief.]
		[Road to Emmaus. J explains prophecies. J seen by Peter.]			[Appearance to 2 disciples. They report. Disbelief.]
	[Peter & BD go to tomb. BD believes. Both go home.]				
			Women report to apostles.		
	MM sees 2 angels.				

ACTS	JOHN	LUKE	MATTHEW	MARK A	MARK B
			[Guards tell priests: body stolen.]		
	[MM sees gardener = J. Tell apostles J going to Father.]				
	Appearance to apostles in Jerusalem.	Appearance to apostles in Jerusalem. Touch and eating. J explains prophecies.			Appearance to apostles in Jerusalem. Rebuke.
	Mission + Holy Spirit in Jerusalem.	Mission + Holy Spirit. Stay in Jerusalem.			Mission [& promise of charisma] in Jerusalem.
	[Thomas absent.]				
	[Thomas present.]				
	Sea of Galilee. J unrecognized. Peter confirmed.		Appearance to apostles in Galilee: belief and disbelief. Mission.		
Ascension from Mt of Olives 40 days on.		Ascension from Bethany.			Ascension from Jerusalem.

12

The resurrection of Jesus in the Acts of the Apostles

Our examination of the sayings relating to the resurrection and to the topic of eternal life attributed to Jesus in the Gospels without necessarily implying bodily revival has turned up a surprisingly small amount of material. Afterlife did not seem to have occupied a central position in the thought of Jesus. Perhaps the most likely explanation for this absence is that during his ministry Jesus' eyes were so galvanized on the imminent arrival of the kingdom of God that both he and his followers assumed the transition between their era and the age of the kingdom of God to entail no passing through death. It was only during the brief period separating the cross from the almost instantly expected glorious return of Christ, a period during which some believers would inevitably pass away (1 Thess 4:13–17), that the problem of their resurrection would arise (see pp. 123–5).

The subject of the resurrection gains importance through the treatment of two aspects of the life of Jesus in the Gospels. To serve the apologetical needs of the Church in explaining the cross and the subsequent rising of the Messiah, the evangelists felt obliged to insert into their account of the final phase of the life of Jesus repeated predictions of his coming death and resurrection (see chapter 8). These prophecies apparently aimed at preparing

Jesus' closest associates for his unanticipated downfall and exaltation at the end of his career. It is obvious that in attempting to report the resurrection of Jesus, the evangelists faced an uphill task. Their accounts display numerous inconsistencies. Yet the seven or eight decades – the years between AD 30 and AD 100–110 that separate the death of Jesus from the completion of John's Gospel – witnessed a steadily increasing certainty in the early Church regarding the resurrection of Jesus and his spiritual presence among his followers.

Chronologically, the earliest comments are those of St Paul, whose literary activity extended over the fifties and possibly the early sixties of the first century. Nevertheless, the ideas attributed to the beginnings of the Jesus movement in Jerusalem and Judaea, chronicled in the Acts of the Apostles, have every probability of mirroring in substance the earliest thoughts of the first Jewish-Christian communities of Palestine. The Book of the Acts represents an ideology which still reflects the freshness and the lack of sophistication of the original Jewish followers of Jesus before Paul conquered the intellectual high ground in the Church and exported his ideology to the non-Jewish world of Syria, Asia Minor, Greece and Italy.

The contribution of the Acts to the development of the doctrine on the resurrection is significant, both in the section centred on the activity of Peter (chapters 1–12) and on that of Paul (chapters 13–28). Attention is focused on two main subjects: the fulfilment of prophecies regarding the ultimate fate of the Messiah, and the witnessing role assigned to the apostles, whose principal task was to prove to their compatriots the reality of the resurrection of Jesus.

If we hold the view that Luke is the author of both

the Third Gospel and the Acts we will not be surprised to discover that the prophetic argument in favour of the resurrection of Jesus is attested in both works. Already in Luke's Gospel, as against Mark, Matthew and John, the prediction of the cross and the resurrection is more emphatically assigned to the prophets of the Old Testament than to Jesus.

In the first speech, placed by Luke on the lips of Peter addressing the assembled Jewish multitude in Jerusalem at the feast of Pentecost, the leader of the apostles was determined to prove from the Psalms that the resurrection had been predestined by God and foretold by 'the prophet' David.[1] Luke uses Psalm 16:10, 'For Thou wilt not abandon my soul to Hades, nor let Thy Holy One see corruption', as one of his main proof texts for the resurrection. Pointing out that these words could not refer to David, who lay buried in his tomb in Jerusalem, Peter asserted that the Psalmist must have foretold the triumph over death of the future Messiah, Jesus Christ.[2] It is worth noting that the resurrection of Jesus was inseparably connected with his exaltation and his sitting at the right hand of the Father (Acts 2:22–36). It was further corroborated by the statement that in Jesus came to fulfilment David's prophecy in Psalm 110:1, 'The Lord [God] said to my Lord [the Messiah], Sit at my right hand' (Acts 2:34). With the resurrection and the glorification of Jesus is coupled the charismatic miracle of the reception of the Holy Spirit from God the Father and its transmission to the apostles by Christ (Acts 2:32).

In Jesus was also realized Psalm 118:22, which metaphorically announced the transformation of the stone rejected by the builders into the essential corner stone of a new edifice, the Church (Acts 4:8–11). Finally, speaking in general terms in the house of the Roman centurion Cornelius, Peter declared that according to the testimony of all the prophets Jesus, empowered by the Holy Spirit, mastered diseases and the Devil not only during his life, but also after being raised by God from the dead (Acts 10:34–43).

The second characteristic concerning the passages under consideration relates to the apostles' role in propagating faith in Christ, 'the Author of life' whom God has raised from the dead (Acts 3:15). 'Witness' and 'to witness' are words that turn up again and again in the first ten chapters of the Acts, and the testimony in question is regularly allied to the manifestation of charismatic power.

Already in Acts 1, the purpose of the election of Matthias to the college of the apostles, replacing the traitor Judas, was to make him (together with the other eleven close associates of Jesus) a *witness* of the resurrection. The choice of the new apostle by casting lots contains the suggestion that the winner was selected by God (Acts 1:26), but the most spectacular example of charisma was revealed at Pentecost when Peter and his companions proclaimed to the crowd: 'This Jesus God raised up, and of that we are all witnesses' (Acts 2:32). Their testimony was prompted, we are given to believe, by the glorified risen Jesus who, sitting at God's right hand, completely transformed his hitherto spineless disciples through the gift of the Holy Spirit (Acts 2:33).

The healing of a lame man in the Temple by Peter and John 'in the name of Jesus of Nazareth' (Acts 3:1–16) was another form of witnessing that Christ had been raised from the dead and was active through Peter and his associates. Even when no details are listed, the way of life of the Jerusalem Church under the guidance of the apostles is depicted as a powerful testimony to the resurrection of Jesus (Acts 4:33). Later, when ordered by the high priest to stop creating trouble through preaching about Christ, Peter and his colleagues affirmed it to be their God-given and Spirit-inspired duty to announce the resurrection and exaltation of Jesus and testify to it by word and deed: 'We are witnesses to these things, and so is the Holy Spirit whom God has given to those who obey him' (Acts 5:32).

Finally, in Caesarea, in the house of the Roman centurion Cornelius, Peter's pronouncement concerning the apparition of the resurrected Jesus to him and his companions and the obligation imposed on them to act as his witnesses, was immediately followed by a major charismatic event, the pouring out of the Holy Spirit over the whole Gentile family of Cornelius that made its members speak in tongues and praise God (Acts 10:34–47).

The writer of Acts was not preoccupied by the resurrection of Jesus as such. A risen Messiah, no longer visibly active in society, would not have made much impact on the audience of the apostles. So they presented the resurrection in context. It was a first step conducive to the exaltation and glorification of Jesus and his enthronement in heaven next to God from where he was to dispense the Holy Spirit through his earthly representatives to the world at large. This is an essentially new portrayal of the resurrection of Jesus in the framework of the charismatic activity of the nascent Church.

No presentation of the resurrection in the Acts can be considered complete without touching on three passages expressing the opinion ascribed to Paul on the matter. They foreshadow the point of view encountered in the Pauline letters. Belief in the dying and rising Christ is the most fundamental tenet of the teaching of Paul. Indeed, he asserted before the Jewish high court that all his troubles with the Temple authorities, dominated by the anti-resurrection Sadducees, arose from his belief in the rising of the dead. As a clever rhetorician, he used to his polemical advantage the disagreement on the subject of the resurrection that he knew existed between the Sadducee and Pharisee members of the Sanhedrin. 'Brethren, I am a Pharisee, a son of Pharisees', he cried out in the council, 'with respect to the hope and the resurrection of the dead I am on trial' (Acts 23:6). Thus all of a sudden the Pharisee councillors turned pro-Paul, apparently declaring, 'We find nothing wrong in this man' and even willing to accept that Paul had a supernatural experience: 'What if a spirit or an angel spoke to him?' (Acts 23:9). Paul later reiterated before Felix, the Roman procurator of Judaea, that his preaching of the resurrection was the main reason for the conflict opposing him to the Jewish leadership (Acts 24:15). Lastly, in the presence of the Jewish king, Agrippa II, Paul once again maintained that the chief accusation levelled against him concerned his hope in the resurrection (Acts 26:8) and his teaching that Christ's rising from the dead was the anticipation of the general resurrection (Acts 26:23).

Such is the new perspective opened by the Acts of the Apostles on the resurrection of Jesus. It was the inward motor that propelled the budding Church to preach the Gospel to Jews and Gentiles. This idea now needs to be followed up by the more personal testimony relating to the resurrection contained in the letters of St Paul. It conveys not the tradition handed down by the companions of Jesus during his lifetime, as the Book of the Acts purports to do, but the insights of the great visionary at the gate of Damascus, whose perceptions were to lay the foundations of fully-fledged Christianity.

13

The resurrection of Jesus in Saint Paul

The difference between the approaches to the resurrection in the Gospels and the rest of the New Testament is principally due to the varying stances taken by their writers. As we have seen, the purpose of the evangelists was three-fold. They sought to present the teaching of Jesus about the resurrection and eternal life; to list the predictions made by himself or by the ancient prophets of his death and rising; and to outline the events that happened before dawn on the first Easter Sunday. The other New Testament authors endeavoured to derive from the resurrection story doctrines concerning Jesus and his followers. Put differently, Luke in the Acts, Paul and the rest of the letter writers of the New Testament, took the rising of Christ for granted and endeavoured to describe the impact of the resurrection on the theological understanding of Jesus, or on the apostles and the first Christians.

Saint Paul played a crucial role in establishing resurrection as the kernel of the Christian message. We have already seen that in the Acts Paul's perception of the death and resurrection was the focus of the religion preached by him. More than once he identified his doctrinal outlook as hope founded on the resurrection. He comments only once on the events surrounding the resurrection of Jesus when he passes on to his flock in Corinth a tradition he has inherited from his seniors in the faith concerning the death, burial and resurrection of Jesus:

For I delivered to you as of first importance what I also received, that Christ died for our sins in accordance with the scriptures, that he was buried, that he was raised on the third day in accordance with the scriptures, and that he appeared to Cephas, then to the twelve. Then he appeared to more than five hundred brethren at one time, most of whom are still alive, though some have fallen asleep. Then he appeared to James, then to all the apostles. Last of all ... he appeared also to me (1 Cor 15:3–8).

The tradition received by Paul includes features which are absent from the other resurrection accounts of the New Testament. In his detailed list, there are several otherwise unattested apparitions, such as the vision of the risen Jesus at some unspecified place and time by more than five hundred followers, most of whom were still alive in AD 53 or thereabouts, when Paul wrote his first letter to the Corinthians. He refers to subsequent appearances of Christ to Cephas-Peter and James, the two dominant figures of the primitive Church and the only two apostles whom Paul decided to meet on his first visit to the Jewish-Christian community in Jerusalem. He adds also his own vision of Jesus, no doubt his mystical experience outside Damascus (Acts 9:3–4).[1] It is noteworthy that, although Paul refers to the burial of Jesus, he does not know or wish to mention the discovery of the empty tomb and the disappearance of the body of Christ.

While his report, written in the fifties of the first century, predates Mark, Matthew and Luke by some fifteen to forty-five years, it could well reflect a revised and edited version of events influenced by Paul's 'political' considerations. By asserting that he, too, was granted an appearance of the risen Jesus, Paul intended to insinuate his equality to Peter and James. Also, by omitting to mention the legally worthless female testimony about the empty tomb and the first apparitions of the resurrected Christ to women, he meant to strengthen the evidence coming from reliable male witnesses – Peter, James, Paul himself and a large group of men – many of whom could still be interviewed by any Corinthian pilgrim to the Holy Land keen enough to seek out the survivors. It would seem, however, that when Paul wrote the epistle, the debate was not about the validity of the tradition concerning the resurrection of Jesus, but about the idea prevalent in the Hellenistic world that the return from Hades was meaningless. 'How can some of you say', Paul indignantly inquired, 'that there is no resurrection of the dead?' (1 Cor 15:12).

1. Paul's teaching on the resurrection in 1 Thessalonians

A careful look at Paul's texts reveals that the issue of the resurrection of Jesus did not arise from either historical consideration or from philosophical reflection, but from lively debates in the Pauline communities about the practical sequels of the faith in resurrection. It was connected with the conviction that the dead would rise at the impending *Parousia*, or return of Christ.

Resurrection linked to the *Parousia* arose in the early stages of Paul's literary activity as it is attested in the first letter to the Thessalonians between AD 50 and 52. The eyes of the faithful in the Church of Thessalonica were focussed on the imminent coming from heaven of Christ, the Son of God, risen from the dead and deliverer of the faithful from judgement (1 Thess 1:9–10; see also 2 Cor 4:14; 5:14–15).

The eschatological enthusiasm generated by the expectation of the *Parousia* produced, Paul tells us, extravagant ideas among the Thessalonians. Some of them went so far as to proclaim that the Lord had already arrived and his return had been announced in a letter by Paul himself (2 Thess 2:1–2).[2]

The Thessalonians were eagerly awaiting the great event, but some of them expressed concern about the fate of those Church members who had died before the day of Christ's return. Paul reassured them: as God raised Christ, he would also revive the dead who had believed in the risen Jesus. His resurrection holds the key to salvation. Paul then presented the following scenario of the *Parousia*: The Lord Jesus would descend from heaven and order an archangel to sound the trumpet for resurrection. Then 'the dead in Christ' would return to life and be lifted up by clouds, vehicles of heavenly transport, to meet Jesus in the air, while the living Christians, including Paul himself, without passing through death would be caught up with them and join Jesus and remain with him for ever. In short, Paul and his early followers envisaged the resurrection of Jesus first and foremost as the prototype and cause of the rising of the dead and as the source and guarantee of the eternal salvation of all the chosen.

But we would not have you ignorant, brethren, concerning those who are asleep . . . For since we believe that Jesus died and rose again, even so, through Jesus, God will bring him to those who have fallen asleep. For this we declare to you by the word of the Lord, that we who are alive, who are left until the coming of the Lord, shall not

precede those who have fallen asleep. For the Lord himself will
descend from heaven, with a cry of command, with the archangel's
call, and with the sound of the trumpet of God. And the dead in
Christ will rise first; then we who are alive, who are left, shall be
caught up together with them in the clouds to meet the Lord in the
air; and so we shall always be with the Lord (1 Thess 4:13–17).

While on this occasion the beneficial effects of Christ's
resurrection were seen as affecting only deceased Church
members, a few years later in the mid-AD 50s the perspective broadened. After a short while, in his first correspondence with the Corinthians, Paul mentions the curious
custom of Christians undergoing baptism on behalf of
the dead. The vicarious rite was intended to ensure that
deceased pagans close to Church members might draw
some benefit from the resurrection of Jesus.

Since for Paul the resurrection of Jesus was the token
of the future resurrection of the baptized, his theory
applied only to a tiny portion of the dwellers in Sheol, a
handful of dead Christians and a few pagans redeemed
through the baptism for the dead. Paul's perspective did
not include all the righteous who had died before Christ,
let alone the resurrection of all the just and the wicked
since Adam.

2. Paul's teaching on the resurrection in
1 Corinthians

Paul's preoccupation with the problem of the resurrection
did not come to an end with the first letter to the Thessalonians, but revealed itself to be especially lively in the first
letter to the Corinthians. Indeed, chapter 15 of that letter

provides the most detailed record of Paul's understanding of the impact of the resurrection of Jesus on Christian believers. Here again Paul confronts a theological problem from a practical point of view. He condemned Christian men frequenting prostitutes because he perceived a mystical union between the human body and the body of Christ. In his view, the bodies of the faithful belonged to the Lord. Having died with the crucified Christ when they were dipped into the baptismal pool, their flesh was symbolically raised with the risen Christ when they emerged from the water. Hence Paul's negative answer to the question, 'Shall I take the members of Christ and make them members of a prostitute? Never' (1 Cor 6:15).

The same letter speaks of members of the Church querying the possibility of the resurrection of the dead. For Paul, this was tantamount to a denial of the resurrection of Christ and of the faith he had preached. If the dead cannot be raised, he argues, then Jesus was not raised. Consequently, sins are still unredeemed, hope in the resurrection is futile, and all the deceased Christians are lost (1 Cor 15:12–18). However, he continues, the resurrection of Jesus was not for his own sake alone, but being 'the first fruits' of all those to be raised, it marked the beginning of a multitude of reawakenings. As the first Adam inflicted death on all his posterity, the risen Christ mystically enabled those who were to believe in him to have a share in life through his resurrection (1 Cor 15:20–23).

As a Jew, Paul could not conceive of resurrection without envisaging some kind of a body, but, combining his Jewish legacy with the Hellenistic ideas of his readers, he insisted that this body would be totally different from the one that had died. The risen body would be imperishable, glorious and powerful, bearing the image not of the mortal

Adam, but that of the glorified Christ. The raised dead would be granted a spiritual body, and the just, alive at the *Parousia*, would have their earthly bodies transformed into spiritual ones:

We shall not all sleep, but we shall all be changed, in a moment, in the twinkling of an eye, at the last trumpet. For the trumpet will sound, and the dead will be raised imperishable, and we shall be changed. For this perishable nature must put on the imperishable, and the mortal nature must put on immortality (1 Cor 15:51–54).

In sum, in his address to the Corinthians, Paul did not seek to clarify the meaning of Jesus' resurrection, but its effects on his followers. The resolution of the significance of the resurrection as far as Jesus himself was concerned had to wait until Paul's later correspondence, especially until the epistle to the Romans.

3. Paul's teaching on the resurrection in the letter to the Romans

Writing to the Romans in the mid or late AD 50s, Paul reflected on the resurrection considered from the angle of Christ's relation to God and to the community of believers. Unlike John, who in the Prologue of his Gospel identified Jesus as the eternal divine Word become human for a short time, Paul, moving in the opposite direction, solemnly declared that the man Jesus, born of a Jewish woman as a descendant of King David, rose to the dignity of the Son of God through his resurrection from the dead (Rom 1:4). In other words, on the first Easter Sunday the status of Jesus underwent a fundamental change. The opening paragraph of the letter to the Romans marks the moment in the history of Christian literature when Jesus was formally proclaimed 'Son of God in power according to the Spirit of holiness' on account of his resurrection from the dead.

In the same way, Paul also emphasized the role of the resurrection in the relationship between Jesus and his followers. He expressed his thought through the medium of the mystical, or sacramental, concept of baptism. Paul did not view baptism merely as a Jewish rite of purification by water. For him the pool symbolized the tomb where the body of Jesus had lain and where the resurrection took place. So when the candidates to be initiated into the Christian mystery were submerged in the baptismal waters, they mystically united themselves with the sin-effacing death of Christ. Afterwards, when they rose from the pool, they believed they started a new life issued from the resurrection of Jesus and became children of God.

Do you not know that all of us who have been baptized into Christ Jesus were baptized into his death? We were buried therefore with him by baptism into death, so that as Christ was raised from the dead by the glory of the Father, we too might walk in newness of life (Rom 6:3–4; *cf.* Col 2:12).

This birth to a new life was animated by the Spirit of God emanating from the resurrection of Jesus.

If the Spirit of him who raised Jesus from the dead dwells in you, he who raised Christ Jesus from the dead will give life in your mortal bodies also through the Spirit which dwells in you (Rom 8:11).

A little later on, the centrality of the resurrection in the life of the faithful is expressed with even more emphatic succinctness: 'If you confess with your lips that Jesus is Lord and believe in your heart that God raised him from the dead, you will be saved' (Rom 10:9).

Apart from the correspondence with the Thessalonians, Corinthians and Romans, the theme of the resurrection from the dead plays little or no part in the rest of the Pauline and deutero-Pauline literature.[3] The epistles to the Galatians, Ephesians, Philippians, Colossians, 2 Timothy and Hebrews use the terms 'resurrection' and 'to rise' only ten times, adding nothing to the meanings with which we are already familiar. The other letters, 1 Timothy, Titus and Philemon, never broach the subject.

One final point needs to be examined before concluding the discussion of Paul's contribution to the topic of the resurrection of Jesus. In 1 Corinthians 15:3 Paul firmly asserts that Jesus rose from the dead on the third day 'in accordance with the scriptures', yet contrary to his custom, he fails to back his statement with a citation. It is possible that the post-biblical Jewish representation of Genesis 22, the voluntary self-sacrifice of Isaac, in which the death and the resurrection of the victim on Mount Moriah is figuratively contemplated, kept on haunting Paul's creative imagination.[4] However, only the deutero-Pauline letter to the Hebrews furnishes positive support to this theory.

By faith Abraham . . . offered up Isaac . . . He considered that God was able to raise men even from the dead; hence, figuratively speaking, he received him back (Heb 11:17–19).

Nevertheless, the absence of an actual Bible quotation in favour of the resurrection of the Messiah suggests that there existed no established tradition among Jews about a dying and risen Christ.

In sum, whereas the idea of the resurrection lay at the periphery of the preaching of Jesus, based on the idea of the kingdom of God, St Paul turned it into the centrepiece of his mystical and theological vision, which was soon to become quasi-identical with the essence of the Christian message.

The resurrection of Jesus in the rest of the New Testament

The remaining books of the New Testament contribute remarkably little to the problem of the resurrection. The letters of James, 2 Peter, 1–3 John and Jude are silent on the subject. Only the first epistle of Peter has something new to say and the Book of Revelation contains a single reference to general resurrection.

To begin with the latter, chapter 20 of Revelation offers an idiosyncratic picture of the resurrection with no parallel anywhere in the New Testament. Unlike the Hebrew Bible and post-biblical Jewish literature, it depicts the general raising of the dead not in one, but in two stages. The first resurrection is linked to the return of Christ and benefits only the martyrs, 'those who had been beheaded for their testimony to Jesus'. According to the imagery of Christian millenarian speculation, they are to reign with Christ for a thousand years, during which 'the dragon, that ancient serpent, who is the Devil and Satan', will be bound and imprisoned (Rev 20:2–4). At the end of the millennium comes the second resurrection (Rev 20:5), that of the rest of mankind, both the pious and the impious of the past ages, followed by the last judgement. Those inscribed in God's book of life are to join the beneficiaries of the first resurrection, and the wicked will be condemned to a second death and cast for ever into a lake of fire (Rev

20:11–15). This two-tier concept of resurrection has never become part of mainstream Christian thinking, but inspired esoteric speculations over the centuries.

The first letter of Peter also includes something unattested elsewhere, called the 'harrowing of hell' in English theological jargon; that is to say Christ's descent to the underworld between his death and resurrection in order to rescue the deceased. The idea is associated with the redeeming symbolism of a new birth springing from the resurrection of Jesus (1 Pet 1:3). The principal passage contains an explicit hint at baptism.

For Christ also died for sins once and for all . . . that he might bring us to God, being put to death in the flesh but made alive in the spirit, in which he went and preached to the spirits in prison, who formerly did not obey, when God's patience waited in the days of Noah, during the building of the ark, in which a few, that is eight persons, were saved through water. Baptism, which corresponds to this, now saves you, not as a removal of dirt from the body but as an appeal to God for a clear conscience, through the resurrection of Jesus Christ, who has gone into heaven and is at the right hand of God, with angels, authorities, and powers subject to him (1 Pet 3:18–22).

The letter resumes the main features of the theological canvas of redemption familiar from the writings of Paul: Christ's death expiated man's sin and his resurrection brought about the salvation of the believer through baptism. The novel element in the picture is the saving action that the dead, but already spiritually revived Jesus, performed in the underworld prior to his terrestrial resurrection. Some time between the afternoon of Good Friday and the dawn of Easter Sunday, Jesus visited Sheol, the abode of the deceased, intending to save a special group of sinners. They were the wicked humans of the age of the flood, who failed to amend their ways during the time of repentance granted them by a magnanimous God, while Noah was building the ark. According to Jewish tradition, God would not decree the destruction of this most dissolute of all generations without giving them a chance to repent. Hence Noah, who is described as the 'herald of righteousness' (2 Pet 2:5), was ordered to preach to them and try to bring them to their senses before it was too late.[1] He was not listened to, so all mankind perished except 'eight souls' – Noah and his wife, his three sons and their three wives – who escaped destruction in the ark. The water that carried the ark prefigured baptism and its saving power derived from the resurrection of Christ. We are not told whether Jesus, already filled with the Spirit, was more successful than Noah, but the episode underlines the universal character of the redeeming intention attributed to him by the writer of 2 Peter.

The main novelty of the story is the insertion of a new stage into the sequence of events between the death and the resurrection of Christ: the journey to hell of the soon rising, but not yet risen, Jesus and the extension of his saving gesture to all the deceased, represented by the worst of sinners. This enlarged aim far exceeds Paul's restricted purpose, which was the communication of the fruits of the resurrection to the dead Christians. This generosity of 1 Peter towards the deceased of all ages is remembered by the introduction of this odd detail of the story of Jesus into some of the Church's Creeds. The Apostles' Creed reads: 'He suffered under Pontius Pilate, was crucified, died and was buried, descended to hell, rose from the dead on the third day.'

The Athanasian Creed, in turn, declares: 'Who suffered

for our salvation, descended to hell, rose from the dead on the third day.'

Appendix

'Life' and 'eternal life' in the New Testament outside the Gospels

Our analysis in chapter 7 of the use of 'life' or 'eternal life' has shown that in the Synoptics the terms are synonymous with the 'kingdom of God', and 'eternal life' is seen as the reward for the observance of God's commandments and even more so for the performance of heroic virtue. In the Gospel of John, on the other hand, eternal life is the ultimate remuneration for faith in Jesus, the Son of God. None of the evangelists ever explicitly links resurrection with eternal life. The latter can be conceived of without the idea of bodily revival. If one is to distinguish between 'life' and 'eternal life', the former would indicate the granting of circumstances that lead towards the kingdom of God, whereas the latter is the prerogative of the established citizens of that kingdom.

Paul frequently refers to 'life' or 'eternal life', but he does so without explicitly alluding either to the resurrection of Jesus or to resurrection in general. Twice he introduces the idea of immortality, seen as a sign of spiritual survival (Rom 2:7; 2 Tim 1:10), but as a rule the main contrast is between death brought by Adam and life originating with Jesus Christ (Rom 5:17–18, 20; 6:23). Paul comes nearest to associating life with resurrection when he depicts human bodies as vehicles carrying both the death of the crucified Jesus and the life of the risen Christ (2 Cor 4:10–11).

The three Johannine letters, which never speak of resurrection, generally agree with the Fourth Gospel in joining the notion of faith to eternal life. As for the Book of Revelation, it is rich in symbols such as 'water of life' (Rev 7:17; 21:6, 22:1, 17), 'tree of life' (Rev 2:7; 22:2, 14, 19), 'crown of life' (Rev 2:10; cf. Jas 1:12) and 'book of life' (Rev 3:5; 13:8; 17:8; 20:12, 15; 21:27; cf. Phil 4:3).

All in all, these passages regarding 'eternal life' contribute little to the interpretation of the notion of resurrection.

The meaning of the concept of resurrection in the New Testament

After the survey of the biblical and post-biblical Jewish evidence concerning afterlife and the examination of the full New Testament material, what have we learnt about the early Christian concept of the resurrection of the dead in general, and the resurrection of Jesus in particular?

Let it be emphasized once again that most of the Old Testament ignores the idea of the revivification of the dead; that active and effective religious life is seen by ancient Judaism as restricted to man's worldly career and that the inevitability of death and a permanent Sheol entailing a reduced, joyless and as it were Godless existence in a dreamless sleep is accepted as mankind's inexorable heritage.

Yet, while in biblical wisdom this world and the present age are the theatre of the love and worship of God, one detects in Jewish piety of the later centuries of the Old Testament era a secret yearning for a continued relationship after death with the Creator and heavenly Father. We have to wait, however, until the end of the third and early second centuries BC, and in particular until the Jewish experience of religious martyrdom, to encounter the notion of life after death in the form of spiritual immortality or bodily revival. These concepts had been attested, especially under the influence of the Pharisees, from the second century BC onwards, but they do not seem to have become part of the core of Judaism until the second or third century AD and later. Since in the early first century AD the impact of the Pharisees on Galilee was at best limited, the frequently assumed notion that belief in resurrection was an accepted fact among the contemporaries of Jesus cannot be derived from sources reflecting popular traditions current in the Judaism of that age.

As the relevant findings have been listed in passing in the foregoing chapters dealing with the New Testament, all that remains here is to offer a systematic exposition of the meaning of resurrection. This will be done under three headings. The first two relate to theology, but the third will take us to the heart of the matter, the 'event' of the resurrection of Jesus.

Before addressing these three issues, a preliminary question must be settled. How do the various accounts of resurrection, or rather resuscitation, mentioned in the Old and New Testaments (see pp. 30–32 and chapter 9) compare with the resurrection of Jesus and with the eschatological resurrection envisaged for mankind?

Resuscitation is the 'miraculous' continuation of life as it was lived previously, the climax of charismatic healing. By contrast, the rising of the dead (with the exception of the wandering about of 'the saints' in Jerusalem after the earthquake that marked the death of Christ (see pp. 92–3), is considered as an occurrence awaited in the future. It is associated with the expected Second Coming or *Parousia*, and the accompanying universal, final judgement of all mankind which conclude the present age. As for the resurrection of Jesus, it is depicted as a unique phenomenon, both historical and eschatological. It is not seen as the continuation of Jesus' pre-crucifixion life, nor is his resurrected body represented as identical with the one known to his companions. Moreover, his resurrection is treated as the anticipation and cause of the reawakening of the dead at the end of time. In short, the resumed existence of the resuscitated dead brought about by Elijah, Elisha, Jesus, Peter and Paul sheds no true light on the concept of eschatological resurrection. The two fall into separate categories.

1. The significance of the resurrection for the theological understanding of Jesus by nascent Christianity

Contrary to the generally held opinion that the concept of resurrection constitutes the focal point of Christology, the doctrine relating to Jesus, close scrutiny of the New Testament evidence suggests that it forms simply the initial stage of the belief in his exaltation. Christ's complete glorification is seen in his enthronement next to God the Father in fulfilment of the words of the Psalmist, 'The Lord said to my Lord, Sit at my right hand' (Acts 2:24, 32–34, quoting Ps 110:1).

The Gospel of John also gives the impression that the resurrection was simply the gateway through which the incarnate eternal Word of God returned to the Father after the accomplishment of his temporary earthly mission. In his first appearance to Mary Magdalene, Jesus immediately announces that he is going to the Father (Jn 20:17). This turning point in his mission is revealed in the general statement that sums up John's Gospel: 'I came from the Father and have come into the world; again, I am leaving the world and going to the Father' (Jn 16:28). His heavenly homecoming was soon marked by the charismatic pouring out of the Holy Spirit over the apostles, left behind as the witnesses of Jesus.

The same idea is voiced by St Paul, for whom the resurrection is the cause of Jesus' elevation to divine Sonship (Rom 1:4). In short, the apogee of the triumphant Christ is not the rising from the dead, but his heavenly exaltation followed by the dispatch of the Holy Spirit.

2. The resurrection of Jesus in relation to the resurrection of his followers and of the rest of mankind

The resurrection does not appear to have had a major doctrinal impact on the Gospels. Neither the general background material, nor the teaching ascribed to Jesus on the afterlife, is particularly concerned with the matter. Paul is the first to raise the question, but he does so more from a pragmatic than from a theoretical viewpoint. In the early stages of the expectation of the return of Christ, the eschatologically frenzied communities of believers were chiefly interested in their own entry into the kingdom of God by means of a forthcoming encounter with Jesus returning from heaven on a cloud. They were convinced that the *Parousia* was at hand and would happen within their lifetime. They would witness it before their death. All they expected therefore was in effect a change of clothes, the divesting of themselves from their earthly frame and replacing it with a new spiritual body. The resurrection as such did not concern them.

But the problem became a burning issue in connection with the members of the Church who died recently. Did they miss the boat? As such injustice seemed inconceivable, Paul reassured the members of his congregation that on D-day the deceased Christians would join the rest of the living followers of Jesus in their triumphant ascent to the divine kingdom. The supplementary ticket issued to this group of Christians who predeceased the *Parousia* was immediately followed by a request for another, and entitlement to resurrection was extended to pagan associates for whom virtual Church membership was secured through the surrogate ritual of baptism for the dead. However, Paul himself did not explicitly apply the power of Jesus' resurrection to the non-baptized righteous of the pre-Christian age. We have to wait until the first letter of Peter for the extension of the saving plan of Christ in regard to the deceased wicked imprisoned in the underworld (see pp. 132–3).

The New Testament remains divided on the final destiny of the ungodly, namely whether they would be raised to face divine justice and eternal hellfire. The resurrection, when conceived as the reward for holy behaviour, was necessarily confined to saints and martyrs, to the just in general, and the wicked were left behind in the cold of Sheol. It was only when some New Testament writers substituted for the loving and forgiving heavenly Father an iron-fisted Judge that the sinners of the underworld were also summoned to be bodily present before the heavenly tribunal to receive a sentence of destruction in the everlasting flames.[1]

3. What does the New Testament tell us about the 'event' of the resurrection of Jesus?

We have now reached the principal topic of this book, *the* Resurrection. No New Testament text attempts to describe the actual return to life of the dead Jesus. All we have are bits of circumstantial evidence, if they can be called evidence, divided into two classes.

The first entails various accounts of female witnesses who, on the third day after the crucifixion, discovered an empty tomb. They thought it was the tomb of Jesus and their finding was later confirmed by two male apostles. Only one explanation of the empty tomb is offered in the Synoptic Gospels: the absence of the body of Jesus was due to his resurrection. It is based on the testimony heard by the women from one or two mysterious strangers (angels?). In John, on the other hand, the disappearance of the body is attributed both by Mary Magdalene and by Peter to the interference of an unknown third party and not to a supernatural event.

The second category of circumstantial evidence is given in all the Gospels except the shorter ending of Mark. It consists of a series of apparitions to various individuals (Mary Magdalene, Peter, James, Paul) or groups (several women, two disciples at Emmaus, seven, ten or eleven apostles, or over five hundred brethren) at various times (on Easter Sunday, the following Sunday or on later dates) and in various places (in Jerusalem, at Emmaus, on a Galilean mountain or by the sea of Tiberias). The meaning of the visions is not obvious: no one realizes at first that the appearing person is Jesus. They variously speak of a ghost or the 'gardener' or a stranger. Thomas is said to have declined to believe his fellow apostles until he experienced by touch the wounds of the resurrected Jesus, and several apostles on the Galilean mountain continued to harbour doubts concerning the reality of their vision of Jesus.

The empty tomb and the apparitions are never directly associated to form a combined argument. For some modern Gospel interpreters the empty tomb saga is 'an apologetic legend' (R. Bultmann), a secondary attempt to provide some 'factual' support to back individual or collective visions. The fragility of the theory is exposed by its intrinsic weakness. The evidence furnished by female witnesses had no standing in a male-dominated Jewish society. In fact, according to Luke, the apostles poked fun at the women. Furthermore, the identity and number of the witnesses differ in the various Gospels as does their testimony. Yet it is clearly an early tradition. If the empty tomb story had been manufactured by the primitive Church to demonstrate the reality of the resurrection of Jesus, one would have expected a uniform and foolproof account attributed to patently reliable witnesses.

To put it bluntly, not even a credulous non-believer is likely to be persuaded by the various reports of the resurrection; they convince only the already converted. The same must be said about the visions. None of them satisfies the minimum requirements of a legal or scientific inquiry. The only alternative historians are left with in their effort to make some sense of the resurrection is to fall back on speculation, hopefully on enlightened speculation.

Six theories to explain the resurrection of Jesus

One could speak of eight theories, but I have discounted the two extremes which are not susceptible to rational judgement: the blind faith of the fundamentalist believer and the out of hand rejection of the inveterate sceptic. The fundamentalists accept the story, not as written down in the New Testament texts, but as reshaped, transmitted and interpreted by Church tradition. They smooth down the rough edges and abstain from asking tiresome questions. The unbelievers, in turn, treat the whole resurrection story as the figment of early Christian imagination. Most inquirers with a smattering of knowledge of the history of religions will find themselves between these two poles. Some of the explanations of the resurrection are insinuated in the Gospels, others emerge from ancient or more recent history. Let us examine them one by one.

1. The body was removed by someone unconnected with Jesus

According to the Gospel of John, the emptiness of the tomb discovered by Mary Magdalene and later confirmed by Peter and the 'beloved disciple', is at first ascribed to unknown persons. Interference with graves was not unusual, as can be deduced from the curse put on tomb desecrators contained in funeral inscriptions (see pp. 59–60). The circumstances of the burial of Jesus suggest a simple explication. The burial took place in great haste because of the imminent onset of the Sabbath and the body was laid in a new tomb, conveniently situated in a nearby garden (Jn 19:41). It was obviously prepared for someone else. Hence it is not unreasonable to suppose that the person in charge of the burial place – the 'gardener' according to Mary Magdalene (Jn 20:15) – took the first opportunity to move the body of Jesus to another available tomb.

The irregular circumstances of Jesus' interment easily account for such an outside intervention. Normally, the funeral duties were carried out by male near kin, but as there is no sign in the Gospel narratives of the presence of the brothers of Jesus at the time of the crucifixion and all his apostles had gone into hiding, one or several less-close acquaintances, Joseph of Arimathea and Nicodemus, stepped in and performed the charitable obligation on Friday afternoon before sunset. According to John, Nicodemus brought along a large quantity of myrrh and aloes to anoint the dead body. Consequently, contrary to the evidence of the Synoptics, there was no need for Jesus' women friends to visit the tomb at the start of the new week to complete the unfinished funerary rituals.

The innocent transfer of the body of Jesus developed later into the legend of the resurrection. However, the fact that the organizer(s) of the burial was/were well known and could have easily been asked for and supplied an explanation, strongly militates against this theory.[2]

2. The body of Jesus was stolen by his disciples

An emphatic rebuttal of the reality of the resurrection is attributed in the Gospel of Matthew to the priestly leaders of Jerusalem. Allegedly, they spread the rumour, which many decades after the death of Jesus was still circulating among the Jewish population of Jerusalem, that the body of Jesus was spirited away by his disciples to produce the semblance of a miraculous resurrection. This story presupposes that a fraudulent prophecy concerning Jesus' rising from the dead was widely known among Palestinian Jews. However, if the closest associates of Jesus did not expect him to rise, it is hard to imagine that outsiders were aware of a prediction, uttered by Old Testament prophets or by Jesus, about his resurrection shortly after his death. The tale of a mischief perpetrated by the apostles is no doubt a later Jewish gossip circulating in Palestine in the time when Matthew wrote his Gospel. Its value for the interpretation of the resurrection is next to nil.

3. The empty tomb was not the tomb of Jesus

The first two explanations are expressly hinted at in the Gospels themselves. The next derives from more subtle allusions underlying the Synoptics. Mark, Matthew and Luke firmly stress that the Galilean women knew where Jesus was buried. While all the cowardly male disciples kept out of sight, the two Marys (Mk and Mt) or the Galilean women (Lk) watched the burial party led by Joseph of Arimathea (Mk 15:47; Mt 27:61; Lk 23:55). Bearing in mind the attitude of male superiority adopted by the apostles on hearing the report of female witnesses about the empty tomb (Lk 24:11), it strikes as most likely that they suspected that Mary Magdalene and her friends had gone to the wrong tomb. If the rock cavity into which the corpse of Jesus was hurriedly laid was freshly prepared to house someone else's remains, no doubt it was in a location reserved for burials with similar tombs surrounding it. In the semi-darkness of dawn a mistake was easy. A present-day reader would wonder why Peter and his colleagues, who considered the women untrustworthy, did not consult Joseph of Arimathea, who was apparently the owner of the tomb (Mt 27:60). Presumably, in the logic of the Gospel narrative, the apparitions of Jesus soon rendered such an inquiry superfluous. The theory of mistaken identity of the tomb, while not inconceivable, certainly does not impose itself.

4. Buried alive, Jesus later left the tomb

That Jesus survived the crucifixion has been propounded by modern writers and novelists from Hugh J. Schonfield's *The Passover Plot* (1965) and Barbara Thiering's *Jesus the Man* (1992) to *The Da Vinci Code* (2003) by Dan Brown. Less extreme believers in Jesus' survival argue that recovery after crucifixion was possible, as it is attested by Flavius Josephus. In his autobiography, Josephus recalls that on an occasion when he was returning to the capital, he saw many crucified Jews by the roadside. Among them he recognized three of his friends, who were still alive. On his pleading, Titus, the future emperor, promptly ordered them to be taken down and treated by Roman physicians and as a result one of the three survived (*Life*, 420).

Jesus remained on the cross for such a short time that Pilate wondered whether he was truly dead when Joseph of Arimathea asked for his body (Mk 15:44). One may further speculate that the piercing of his side by one of the executioners was a later invention introduced by John (Jn 19:34) to dispel doubts as to whether Jesus was dead. But assuming that a semi-conscious Jesus crept out of the tomb in the darkness of night, what happened to him afterwards? Did he disappear into thin air? Not very likely.

5. The migrant Jesus

The idea of Jesus leaving Judaea after he had recovered from his coma is a relatively modern creation. It is part of the teaching of the Ahmadiyya sect of Islam (formed in the nineteenth century), according to which the revived Jesus left the Holy Land, set out towards the east in search of the lost tribes of Israel, and died in Kashmir in India. In the last century, the rich poetic imagination of Robert Graves brought the post-crucifixion Jesus to Rome.[3] So also did Barbara Thiering's peculiar interpretation of the Dead Sea Scrolls. Her married, divorced and remarried Jesus, father of four children, died of old age in Nero's Rome.[4]

In the absence of real ancient evidence these modern musings need not detain us.

6. Do the appearances suggest spiritual, not bodily, resurrection?

While no apparition of the risen Jesus figures in the original, shorter ending of Mark, the oldest of the Gospels, all the other sources describe numerous visions of Christ by Mary Magdalene (Jn, Mk B), the Galilean women (Mt), the Emmaus disciples (Lk, Mk B), Peter (Lk, Paul), the apostles in Jerusalem on Easter Sunday (Mk B, Lk), one without the presence of Thomas and another, on the following Sunday, in his presence (Jn). Jesus was further seen some days later in Galilee on a mountain by eleven apostles or by seven at the sea of Tiberias (Mt, Jn). Further appearances were witnessed, according to Paul, by more than five hundred brothers, by James, and finally by Paul himself at unspecified times and places.

Four types of vision are listed. 1. In Matthew no concrete

details are given. 2. In John and Luke an unknown ordinary man (the gardener or a traveller) is later recognized as Jesus. 3. Again in Luke and John, a spirit mysteriously enters the apostles' residence despite the locked doors. 4. The ghost later becomes a stranger with flesh and bones, who says he is Jesus and invites the apostles to touch him, and he eats with them.

In order to judge the significance of these appearances, we must try to determine the purpose of the resurrection of Jesus in the mind of the evangelists and Paul. From the fact that no one suggests that he came into contact with people outside the circle of his close followers, we must deduce that for the New Testament writers the resurrection was not meant to enable Jesus to perform any further public act. The forty days' extension of his stay with the apostles, not witnessed by anyone from the outside world, formally contradicts Luke as well as Mark's longer ending (Mk 16:19) as both imply that the Ascension happened on Easter Sunday (Lk 24:50). The alleged need for Jesus' remaining with his disciples to give further instruction about the kingdom of God (Acts 1:3) is rendered superfluous by the promise in John that the Holy Spirit will come to teach them all things (Jn 14:26; 16:13). If this was the case, the resurrection of the crucified Jesus is best seen as the first step on the spiritual ladder that leads to his heavenly glorification (see p. 138). Viewed from this angle, the resurrection becomes a purely spiritual concept without requiring any accompanying physical reality. Spiritual resurrection is best associated with visions and appearances. The strictly Jewish bond of spirit and body is better served by the idea of the empty tomb and is no doubt responsible for the introduction of the notions of palpability (Thomas in John) and eating (Luke and John).

What is the evidential value of such diverse visions perceived by individuals or groups of individuals? In essence, they do not differ from the visions of mystics throughout the centuries. No doubt the New Testament characters believed in the reality of their visions of Jesus. But what about people who were not so privileged and had only the word of 'eyewitnesses' to go by? They depended on a double act of faith: faith in the reliability of the reporters and in the reality of the report. Resurrection as a spiritual entity is appropriately expressed by a vision. Anything more tangible is suspect of hallucination, whether individual or collective.

The theory of spiritual resurrection cancels the need for an empty tomb. The body of a risen but immaterial Jesus could have remained in the tomb, with his bones later collected and put into an ossuary inscribed with the Aramaic name Yeshua bar Yehosef (Jesus son of Joseph). Of course, I do not mean to suggest that the ossuary bearing this name, found at Talpiot in Jerusalem in 1980, and recently made famous by a television documentary, originally contained the remains of the Jesus of the Gospels.[5]

All in all, none of the six suggested theories stands up to stringent scrutiny. Does this mean that the traditional resurrection concept, i.e. the miraculous revival in some shape or form of the dead body of Jesus, is doomed to failure in the rational world of today? Or is there another way out of this conundrum that may offer an explanation, if not for the physical resurrection of Jesus, at least for the birth and survival of Christianity?

Epilogue: Resurrection in the hearts of men

The opening chapter of the Acts of the Apostles takes us to the Mount of Olives, where the apostles of Jesus wave goodbye to their Master. They believe, without comprehending it, that he is no longer in the tomb and is on his way to the Father in heaven. It is of little importance whether this spiritual spectacle was witnessed on the third day after the crucifixion or forty days later. What matters is that within a short time the terrified small group of the original followers of Jesus, still hiding from the public gaze, all at once underwent a powerful mystical experience in Jerusalem on the Feast of Weeks (Pentecost). Filled with the promised Holy Spirit, the pusillanimous men were suddenly metamorphosed into ecstatic spiritual warriors. They proclaimed openly the message of the Gospel, and the charismatic potency, imparted to them by Jesus during his ministry, which had enabled them to preach, heal and expel demons, burst into life again and manifested itself in word and in deed. The formerly terrified fugitives courageously spoke up in the presence of the authorities and healed the sick in public, at the gate of the Temple itself. The reality of the charisma opened the apostles' eyes to the mystery of the resurrection. The spiritual healing power of belief lay at the basis of the teaching, curing and exorcizing ability of Jesus in his life. According to the evangelists, he often told the sick who had been restored to health: 'Your faith has healed you.' During his life, Jesus managed to pass on this spiritual power to his disciples so that they could exclaim with joyful amazement: 'Lord, even the demons are subject to us in your name' (Lk 10:17).

According to the New Testament, the chief act of the resurrected Christ in his heavenly glory was the dispatch of the Holy Spirit. 'This Jesus God raised up', Peter announced to the Jewish crowd in Jerusalem. 'Exalted at God's right hand, and having received from the Father the promise of the Holy Spirit, he has poured it out' over his disciples (Acts 2:32). The impact and guidance of the Spirit empowered the apostles and disciples to act as witnesses of Jesus. They did so through charismatic deeds: 'In my name' – Christ is said to have declared – 'they will cast out demons, they will speak in tongues; they will pick up serpents, and if they drink any deadly thing, it will not hurt them; they will lay their hands on the sick, and they will recover' (Mk16:18).

The scene being set, let us now consider from an existential, historical and psychological point of view the original Galilean followers of Jesus during the short period following the first Easter Sunday. The tale of the empty tomb and the apparitions of the lost Lord momentarily illumined their dark despair with a ray of hope. Doubts nevertheless lingered on. However, when under the influence of the Spirit their self-confidence revived, prompting them to resume their apostolic mission, they felt increasingly sure that they were not acting alone, but that Jesus was with them. So, when they again started to preach the gospel 'with authority', as their miracle-working teacher did in Galilee; when they realized that in *the name of Jesus* his charisma was working again, their doubts melted away in the inward certainty that the crucified Master was close to them, as in the old days.[1] The helping hand that gave them strength to carry on with their task was the proof that Jesus had risen from the dead.

Nowhere has this inner transformation been more movingly portrayed than in the haunting final paragraph of a famous book, *On the Trial of Jesus*, by my late friend Paul Winter:

Sentence was passed, and [Jesus] was led away. Crucified, dead, and buried, he yet rose in the hearts of his disciples who had loved him and felt he was near. Tried by the world, condemned by authority, buried by the Churches that profess his name, he is rising again, today and tomorrow, in the hearts of men who love him and feel he is near.[2]

The conviction in the spiritual presence of the living Jesus accounts for the resurgence of the Jesus movement after the crucifixion. However, it was the supreme doctrinal and organizational skill of St Paul that allowed nascent Christianity to grow into a viable and powerful resurrection-centred world religion.

Resurrection in the hearts of men may strike a note of empathy even among today's sceptics and cynics. Whether or not they adhere to a formal creed, a good many men and women of the twenty-first century may be moved and inspired by the mesmerizing presence of the teaching and example of the real Jesus alive in their mind.

Notes

Foreword

1. Geza Vermes, *The Passion* (Penguin, London, 2005), p. 116.
2. Geza Vermes, *The Nativity: History and Legend* (Penguin, London, 2006).
3. For faith wrapped in scholarship, see the 800 page-long monumental *The Resurrection of the Son of God* by N. T. Wright, Bishop of Durham (SPCK, London, 2003).
4. For a recent example, see Robert M. Price and Jeffery Jay Lowder, *The Empty Tomb: Jesus beyond the Grave* (Prometheus Books, Amherst, NY, 2005).

Prologue: The Christian notion of resurrection and its antecedents

1. *Natural History*, 7:55, 150.
2. Philostratus, *Life of Apollonius*, 4:45.

2. Death and its sequels in ancient Judaism: Paving the way for resurrection

1. For the exception of 1 Enoch, see pp. 44–5.
2. 'Exploit the present day'.

3. Biblical and post-biblical antecedents of the resurrection and ascension of Jesus

1. According to an ancient Jewish belief, attested in rabbinic literature, the departed soul, still longing to return to the

body, continued to hover over it for three days (GenR 100:7; yYeb 15c). Resurrection on the third day may somehow be connected with this idea.

2. The sequence of events given in the Hebrew Bible is preferable to the account of the Septuagint where it is said that the prophet lowers himself on the boy seven times without sneezing, or to the Aramaic Targum where Elisha, and not the boy, sneezes seven times.

3. A similar resuscitation is attributed by the Hellenist Artapanus to Moses, who by pronouncing into Pharaoh's ears the name of God, caused him to drop dead, only to bring him back to life again (Eusebius, Praep. Ev. 9:27. 24–25).

4. Whilst hailing Elisha as a thaumaturge, Josephus plays down his part in the resuscitation of the son of the widow of Zarephath and attributes the miracle to God, who 'beyond all expectation brought the child back to life' (*Ant* 8:327).

5. This designation derives either from the Latin *metator*, probably signifying an angelic surveyor, or more likely the great scribe who stands beside the divine throne, from the Greek *ho meta thronon*.

5. Jewish attitudes to afterlife in the age of Jesus

1. Reference to the biblical origin of resurrection is missing from some important manuscripts of the Mishnah. To those excluded from the future world are to be added the readers of heretical books and magical healers as well as those who pronounce the sacrosanct name of God, and the Epicurean, someone who despises religion.

2. The population of Palestine in 1926 under the British mandate was 865,000. If we discount that of Transjordan and about 100,000 Bedouin, we arrive at about 600,000 and it is unlikely that the density of the population was higher in the first century AD than shortly after the First World War.

3. Steven Fine, 'A Note on Ossuary Burial and the Resurrection of the Dead in First-Century Jerusalem', *Journal of Jewish Studies* 51 (2000), pp. 69–76.

4. *La croyance des Esséniens en la vie future* I (1993), p. 199.

5. *Ancient Jewish Epitaphs* (1991), p. 114.

6. *Jewish Symbols in the Graeco-Roman Period* IV (1954), pp. 71–98.

7. L. Y. Rahmani, *A Catalogue of Jewish Ossuaries in the Collections of the State of Israel* (Jerusalem, 1994), nos. 815 and 829, figures 127–128.

8. J. B. Frey, *Corpus Inscriptionum Iudaicarum, Vol. I, Europe* (1936), *32, p. 550.

7. The teaching of Jesus on resurrection and eternal life

1. The one significant Synoptic text indicating universal resurrection in view of the reward of the just and the punishment of the wicked is Matthew's story of the last judgement (Mt 25:31–46). It has no parallels among the parables safely attributable to Jesus. To this may be added Mk 9:43–48; Mt 18:8–9; see p. 75.

2. Geza Vermes, *The Authentic Gospel of Jesus* (Penguin, London, 2004), pp. 348–49.

3. Vermes, *The Authentic Gospel of Jesus*, pp. 287–88, 89–90.

4. The expression 'for the gospel' has the same meaning, since it is short for 'for the gospel of the kingdom' (see Mt 4:23 and 24:14 and some ancient manuscripts of Mk 1:14).

5. The four instances (out of twenty-five) where in John eternal life is explicitly connected to raising the dead have been noted earlier in this chapter (see pp. 72–4).

8. Predictions of the resurrection of Jesus

1. John, attempting to reduce the odium incurred by the disciples, claims that Jesus had obtained safe conduct for them from the soldiers sent to arrest him (Jn 18:8).

9. Resurrection accounts in the New Testament regarding persons other than Jesus

1. *Cum* or rather *qum*, as attested in the best ancient manuscripts (Sinaiticus, Vaticanus, etc.), is the incorrect ending of the imperative second person singular. It is the masculine form applied to a feminine subject. This represents the loose Galilean dialect, apparently spoken by Jesus and his associates. Some other codices replace *qum* by the grammatically correct *qumi*, thus trying to improve or make more literate the language used by Jesus.

2. Legends circulating in the Eastern and the Western Church represent Lazarus as bishop of Cyprus, or even as the bishop of Marseilles in Southern France, where he arrived by boat together with his sisters Mary Magdalene and Martha.

10. The Gospel accounts of the resurrection of Jesus

1. For a more detailed discussion of the burial of Jesus see Geza Vermes, *The Passion* (Penguin, London, 2005), pp. 77–116.

2. Possibly the wife of Zebedee and the mother of the apostles James and John: see Mt 27:56).

3. Such an extended earthly stay of the risen Jesus is reasserted in the Acts of the Apostles: 'For many days he appeared to those who came up with him from Galilee to Jerusalem' (Acts 13:31).

4. If authentic, a segment of the Testimonium Flavianum of Josephus may be relevant here as indicating a belief in a kind of spiritual resurrection: 'When Pilate, upon hearing him accused by men of the highest standing amongst us, had condemned him to be crucified, those who had in the first place come to love him did not give up their affection for him' (*Ant* 18:64). To this purportedly genuine statement of Josephus, a Christian interpolator, borrowing from the New Testament, later added: 'On the third day

he appeared to them restored to life, for the holy prophets had foretold this and myriads of other marvels concerning him.' It has been suggested that the apocryphal Gospel of Peter, a Greek composition probably written in the late second century, contains some primary source material. See J. D. Crossan, *The Cross That Spoke: The Origin of the Passion Narrative* (1988). Nevertheless, even a perfunctory glance at the text proves that it is dependent on the canonical Gospels so that its treatment here would be a waste of time.

5. *The Resurrection of the Son of God* (SPCK, London, 2003), pp. 5–6.

6. *Der alte und der neue Glaube* (1872), p. 72.

11. Initial evaluation of the accounts of the resurrection of Jesus

1. Josephus' reference in the Testimonium Flavianum to the resurrection of Jesus is considered by all modern experts as a Christian interpolation. 'On the third day he appeared to them restored to life, for the holy prophets had foretold this and myriads of other marvels concerning him' (*Ant* 18:64).

12. The resurrection of Jesus in the Acts of the Apostles

1. David wears the same prophetic mantle in the Dead Sea Scrolls, where his poems are said to have been 'uttered through prophecy' (11Q Psalms col. 27:11).

2. The same argument, using the same quotation of Ps 16:10, is attributed to Paul in his sermon in the synagogue of Antioch in Pisidia (Acts 13:26–39).

13. The resurrection of Jesus in Saint Paul

1. Little is known about Paul's previous contact with the Jerusalem Church. He speaks of his initial violent hostility

towards the Jesus movement (Gal 1:14) and the Acts of the Apostles refers to his presence at the stoning of the deacon Stephen (Acts 7:58). For a fuller sketch of Paul's career, see Geza Vermes, *The Changing Faces of Jesus* (Penguin, London, 2000), pp. 59–75.

2. In a similar vein, two Church members, Hymenaeus and Philetus, godless chatterers according to Paul, also confused some believers by advancing the view that the resurrection had already occurred (2 Tim 2:16–18).

3. The deutero-Pauline letters, attributed by scholars not to Paul, but to his disciples, include Ephesians, Colossians, Hebrews, and the Pastoral epistles addressed to Timothy and Titus.

4. Vermes, *The Changing Faces of Jesus*, pp. 84–86.

14. The resurrection of Jesus in the rest of the New Testament

1. Josephus, too, is familiar with Noah's attempt to persuade his contemporaries to change their minds. 'But Noah, indignant at their conduct and viewing their counsels with displeasure, urged them to come to a better frame of mind and amend their ways; but seeing that, far from yielding, they were completely enslaved to their pleasure of sin, he feared that they would murder him and, with his wives and sons and his sons' wives, quitted the country' (*Ant* 1:74). The same ideas are also attested in rabbinic literature.

15. The meaning of the concept of resurrection in the New Testament

1. As has been shown in chapter 14, the Book of Revelation advances the idea of double resurrection, the first bestowed on those who sacrificed their lives for Christ and enjoyed renewed existence for a thousand years, and the second affecting the rest of dead mankind who would receive their

just deserts of eternal life or a second death in the lake of fire.

Some Jewish religious thinkers have remained hesitant when faced with the idea of eternal damnation colliding with the concept of a merciful God. A nineteenth-century Russian Jewish legend associated with the saintly Rabbi Hayyim of Volozhin goes so far as to advocate universal salvation. According to this tale, when Rabbi Hayyim died, he was told that he could enter heaven at once. As a true son of Abraham, he began to bargain with God's representative. He first stipulated that all his pupils should also be granted immediate entry, then all the Jews and finally all the Gentiles. The heavenly negotiator could not agree to the last demand on the grounds that God had not yet decided about the coming of the Messiah. So Hayyim decided not to cross the gate of heaven and continued to pray outside until the Almighty agreed to the salvation of the whole human race. See Louis Jacobs, *A Jewish Theology*, (Darton, Longman & Todd, London, 1973), p. 322.

2. Ancient tombs were, of course, often broken into by robbers looking for money, jewels or other valuables. If real, the hundred pounds' weight of precious ointments mentioned in the Fourth Gospel might have seemed attractive to the criminal confraternity of Jerusalem.

3. *Jesus in Rome* (London, 1957), pp. 12–13.

4. *Jesus the Man* (New York, 1992), p. 160.

5. Another epitaph with the carving 'Jesus, son of Joseph' was discovered in 1926 by Eleazar Lipa Sukenik. For the inscriptions see L. Y. Rahmani, *A Catalogue of Jewish Ossuaries in the Collections of the State of Israel*, (Jerusalem, 1994), no. 9; Amos Kloner, 'A Tomb with inscribed ossuaries', *Atiqot* 29 (1996), pp. 15–22; James D. Tabor, *The Jesus Dynasty* (HarperCollins, London, 2006), pp. 22–33.

Epilogue: Resurrection in the hearts of men

1. It is noteworthy that even rabbinic literature records that an early Jewish-Christian, Jacob of Kfar Sama, offered to heal the sick 'in the name of Jesus' (tHullin 2:20–22).
2. *On the Trial of Jesus* (2nd edn., Berlin/New York, 1974), p. 208.

Select bibliography

Allison, Dale C., *Resurrecting Jesus: The Earliest Christian Tradition and its Interpreters* (T. & T. Clark, New York/London, 2005).

Avis, Paul (ed.), *The Resurrection of Jesus Christ* (Darton, Longman & Todd, London, 1993).

Barr, James, *The Garden of Eden and the Hope of Immortality* (SCM Press, London, 1992).

Barton, Stephen and Graham Stanton (eds.), *Resurrection: Essays in Honour of Leslie Houlden* (SPCK, London, 1994).

Brown, Raymond E., *The Virginal Conception and the Bodily Resurrection of Christ* (Paulist Press, New York, 1973).

Bultmann, Rudolf, *History of the Synoptic Tradition* (Blackwell, Oxford, 1963).

Charlesworth, James H., et al. (eds), *Resurrection: The Origin and Future of a Biblical Doctrine* (T. & T. Clark, New York/London, 2006).

Davis, Stephen T., Daniel Kendal and Gerald O'Collins (eds.), *The Resurrection: An Interdisciplinary Symposium on the Resurrection of Jesus* (Oxford University Press, Oxford, 1997).

Dunn, James D. G., *Jesus Remembered* (Wm. B. Eerdmans, Grand Rapids, MI, 2003).

Elledge, K. C. D., *Life after death in early Judaism: the evidence of Josephus* (Mohr Siebeck, Tübingen, 2006).

Evans, C. F., *Resurrection and the New Testament* (SCM Press, London, 1970).

Moule, C. F. D., *The Significance of the Message of the Resurrection for the Faith in Jesus Christ* (SCM Press, London, 1968).

Nickelsburg, George W. E., *Resurrection, Immortality and Eternal Life in Intertestamental Judaism and Early Christianity. Expanded Edition* (Harvard University Press, Cambridge MA, 2006).

Price, Robert M. and Jeffery Jay Lowder (eds.), *The Empty Tomb: Jesus beyond the Grave* (Prometheus Books, Amherst, MA, 2005).

Puech, Émile, *La croyance des Esséniens en la vie future: immortalité, résurrection, vie éternelle? Histoire d'une croyance dans le judaïsme ancien* I–II (Cerf, Paris, 1993).

Segal, Alan F., *Life after death: A History of the Afterlife in Western Religion* (Doubleday, New York, 2004).

Stewart, Robert B. (ed.), *The Resurrection of Jesus: John Dominic Crossan and N. T. Wright in Dialogue* (Fortress Press, Minneapolis, 2006).

Wright, N. T., *The Resurrection of the Son of God* (SPCK, London, 2003).

Index

Joseph of Arimathea, 94, 98, 145, 146
Josephus, Flavius:
    Against Apion by, 51–3
    on ascension of Elijah and Enoch, 34
    on Elisha's miracles, 91
    Jewish Antiquities by, 51–2
    on martyrdom, 44
    on religious attitudes, 46, 48–53, 56,
        91, 146
    resuscitation described by, 32
Judah, 42
Judaism:
    afterlife as desire in, 136–7
    in Babylonian exile, 16
    concept of resurrection in, 5, 6, 32,
        53–4, 126, 129
    death in, 15–16, 20–25, 136
    Final Judgment in, 6–7
    Hellenistic, 47
    menorah of, 58
    Mishnah of, 53
    ossuaries in, 56, 58
    pleasures enjoyed in, 27–8
    in post-exilic period, 18, 29
    rabbinic code of law, 53–4
    and religious martyrdom, 136
    spirit and body bonded in, 148
    value of life in, 27
    women as witnesses in, 111, 123, 141
Judas, martyrdom of, 44

Kingdom of God:
    establishment of, 89
    as eternal life, 75, 76–7, 80, 134
    imminent arrival of, 115, 139
    in Jesus' teachings, 76–7, 80, 148

Lazarus, 8, 74, 90, 112
Leontius, Leo, 59
Luke, Gospel of:
    Resurrection in, 98–100, 117
    see also Synoptic Gospels
Luke, Saint:
    and Acts of Apostles, 103, 117
    on the Sadducees, 48, 69

Maccabean revolution, 5, 29, 37
Maccabees:
    Fourth Book of, 43–4

Second Book of, 41–2, 51
Malachi, 87
Mark, Gospel of:
    longer ending of, 102–103
    Resurrection in, 101–103
    shorter ending of, 101–102
    Sinaitic Syriac translation of, 101
    Sinaiticus, 101
    Vaticanus, 101
    see also Synoptic Gospels
martyrs, resurrection of, 7, 29, 37–8, 41,
    44, 131, 136, 140
Mary (mother of Jesus), visit to the
    tomb, 94, 98, 100–101, 109
Mary Magdalene:
    demons expelled from, 89, 102
    risen Christ unrecognized by, 26, 97,
        141, 147
    visit to the tomb, 94, 96–102, 107,
        109, 138, 141, 145
Masada, 44
Matthew, Gospel of:
    Resurrection in, 100–101, 145
    see also Synoptic Gospels
Matthias, 44, 118
messianic age, onset of, 89
Metatron, 33, 35
Methuselah, 33
Michael, angel, 40
miracles, public acceptance of, 91–2
Mishnah, 53
Moses:
    and brazen serpent, 81, 84
    elevation of, 32, 35
mystics, 149

Nain, young man resuscitated in,
    88–9
Nebuchadnezzar, king of Babel, 17
necromancy, 25–6
Nehemiah, Book of, 55
New Testament:
    Gospels of, *see* Synoptic Gospels
    inconsistencies in, 139–40
    on Jesus' Resurrection, 141–2
    meaning of resurrection in, 136–49
    other books of, 131–5
Nicodemus, 81, 94, 144
Noah, 133